WORD OF

Volume One

Tim Glynne-Jones

For Tali, Tess and Sam

and to you both,
Annaluise & Nigel,

With love,
Tim xx

With thanks to Nick Ovenden,
who designed this book.

First paperback edition published in
Great Britain 2018

Designed by Nick Ovenden
www.nickovenden.com

Printed and bound by CPI Group (UK) Ltd, Croydon, CR0 4YY

Published by Balance Media Ltd
www.balancemedia.co.uk

ISBN: 978-1-912661-00-8

A CIP record of this book is available from
The British Library

INTRODUCTION

It all began, as so few things do, with cheese. Normally cheese comes last, doesn't it? Unless you're making a cheese sandwich, of course, in which case it comes in the middle.

Many books have been written about words. I find most of them rather hectoring. The dictionary, for example. Talk about prescriptive. To me the beauty of words is their ability to bend and mould themselves into new forms, to join up with other words and deliver power, pathos, humour, confusion, anger and love... but above all, meaning. It's the feelings they inspire, the phenomena they describe, the memories they stir, the arguments they ignite...

I'm not in the business of telling people what to do or think, so if you've picked up this book expecting to be told how to use words and how not to use them, put it down again immediately! Now back away slowly and don't give it another thought.

Word of the Week began with no greater ambition than to pass on something mildly interesting once a week via email. Today it has grown into the passing on of something mildly interesting once a week via email and social media. I would like to thank all the people who have opened those emails and responded encouragingly.

For those of you new to Word of the Week, I've included an index. This gives you very little idea of what each entry is about but does at least tell you where to find it. Cheese, you see, wasn't really about cheese at all. It was about... well, read on and you'll find out.

INDEX

1

CHEESE

D o you ever wonder why people in photographs from the Victorian era never seem to be smiling? It could have something to do with scurvy, of course, but the most likely answer is to do with the word 'cheese'.

We all know that 'cheese' is the ideal word for forming the face into a smile for the camera but back in the early years of the last century it was a very different story. The word photographers used to prompt their subjects to pose appropriately was not 'cheese' but 'prunes'.

Yes, prunes.

Why? Try saying it and you'll see. 'Prunes' forces the face into an expression of haughty insouciance, which was very much the order of the day. All that changed between the wars (when people knew only too well the sort of trouble that haughty insouciance could lead to) and looking happy became fashionable. In the 1930s, the invention of the reflex camera triggered a boom in the photography business and by the mid 1940s professional snappers were beginning to tell their subjects to "say cheese".

There is no hard evidence as to who first hit upon this idea but one of the earliest recorded references, in *The Big Spring Herald* of Big Spring, Texas, in 1943, hints that it might have been none other than US President Franklin D. Roosevelt. The paper reports US Ambassador Joseph E. Davies as saying, "Just say 'cheese'. It's an automatic smile. I learned that from a politician." Mr Davies chuckled and added. "An astute politician, a very great politician. But, of course, I cannot tell you who he was…"

The greatest politician Davies served under was Roosevelt, henceforth to be known as The Big Cheese.

2

CARTOGRAPHER

Ever wondered how maps are made? You know, those paper things that look a bit like a giant, fold-out SatNav? As recently as the 1950s, before the days of computerisation, cartographers drew them by hand, working from land survey data and the odd aerial photograph. Here's a picture of a couple of them doing their thing[1]. Everyone looked like Charles Hawtrey in those days.

1935 saw the launch of the great Retriangulation of Great Britain, a campaign by the Ordnance Survey to bring the charted record of the whole nation up to date. This gargantuan task involved sending out surveyors to erect triangulation pillars (Trig Points) atop wind and rain blasted peaks throughout the land.

These beleaguered souls had to work in all conditions, getting soaked through, frozen to the bone and lashed by vicious gales as they lugged the rocks, stones, concrete mix and whatever else was required to build those indestructible triangulation pillars on bleak, remote hilltops. (The sort of task you might associate with Hercules, not Hawtrey). If they were lucky they might be given a horse to help.

It took until 1962 to complete the job. Around 6,000 Trig Points were built in all, enabling those heroic cartographers to map the country with far greater accuracy. So next time you're out rambling with your Ordnance Survey map and you come across a Trig Point, spare a thought for the poor sod who had to get it there, and raise your Thermos to the intrepid cartographer.

3

CABBAGING

If you're already having palpitations about England getting hosed by the Germans again at this year's European Championships, don't watch this video[1]. It shows the triumphant German marbles team beating us at our own game at the 2014 World Marbles Championship. I mention this because tomorrow sees the 84th championship taking place at the Greyhound pub in Tinsley Green, Sussex, as it has done on Good Friday every year since 1932.

An unlikely venue for a world championship, Tinsley Green is a small village on the fringes of Crawley. Look out of your starboard window as you're flying into Gatwick and you might just make it out. But it's a place dripping in history, for they've been playing competitive marbles here since 1538, when two Elizabethan suitors by the names of Giles and Hodge locked horns on the marbles ring for the favour of a local maiden.

The game has rules, of course, which is where 'cabbaging' comes in. Cabbaging is cheating. It's about as despicable as a marbles player can get. One who cabbages is guilty of moving his or her large marble (the tolley) nearer to the target illegally. It's a bit like taking a penalty from 10 yards rather than 12. Now there's a thought…

4

BEE

I learnt an interesting thing this week. Indulge me if this is common knowledge, but I was informed for the first time in my life that a bumblebee and a honeybee are two completely different things. That's right! I don't know about you but I always assumed that the bumblebee was part of the whole honeybee hierarchy, along with workers, drones and queens, but no: bumblebees keep themselves very much apart.

They do make a bit of honey but only for personal consumption. They live in holes in the ground, in much smaller colonies than honeybees (50-400 as opposed to 50,000-60,000) and they can sting more than once. There are 24 different species of bumblebee in the UK but just one species of honeybee.

Which is all by the by because the real question is this: why is a spelling bee so called? The 'spelling' bit is obvious but why a 'bee'? This, of course, is one of those strange terms that has come into English parlance from America but, as with many of those dreadful Americanisms (such as 'faucet' and using Zs instead of Ss), it actually originates from here.

Americans have been using the word 'bee' to mean a gathering or get-together since the 18th century but the word is believed to derive from the Old English 'ben', meaning prayer or favour. From 'ben' came 'bene' and from 'bene' came 'bean', meaning help given by neighbours. From there it was a simple step to knock the 'n' sound off the end and expand the definition to mean a gathering.

Have a buzzing weekend.

5

PURPLE

Not since Robin Hood first donned his Lincoln Green tunic has one man done so much for one colour. The untimely death of Prince has brought purple to the fore today, and what a fine colour he's left us with too, not to mention all that wonderful music.

Ever since Old Testament times, purple has been a regal colour. Nero and Caligula killed for it, the Trojans dipped their horses' tales in it, Odysseus and Penelope slept beneath it on their wedding night and King Solomon decorated the Temple of Jerusalem with it. Favoured by great rulers from Alexander to Catherine to the Emperors of China, not for nothing did Quality Street make their top choc purple.

So why the kudos? As with any commodity, the rarer and harder it is to make, the more valuable and desirable it becomes. Purple was made by the good people of Tyre by gathering thousands of tiny sea snails, shelling them, removing one particular gland, squeezing the juice out of it and leaving it in the sun. In a miraculous transformation, the juice turned from white, to yellow, to green, to red and then darkened to purple, whereupon it was taken out of the sun and applied to fabrics, fleeces and horses' tails.

The dye was not only a lovely vivid colour, it also had excellent holding properties, so it didn't run when the ancients accidentally put it in a hot wash.

In the 15th century, Pope Paul II instigated a fashion shift away from purple to scarlet and the colour fell from grace. At its lowest ebb, the Nazis commandeered purple to identify Jehovah's Witnesses, which brings us back to Prince. A sad loss indeed. Never again will the colour purple be worn with such panache.

6

MANGANESE

This week we have been mostly eating pineapple. Why? Because there's only so much goodness you can get from chocolate and pork pies. And, because we like to take an interest in our food (especially the pork pies), this dietary diversion led to a spot of research into the spiky multifruit.

Multifruit?

That's right. A pineapple isn't one fruit, it's an amalgamation of lots of individual fruits. Each of those tough flaky bits that stick out the side is a fruit in its own right. But that's by the by. The more important discovery was that pineapple is a particularly rich source of manganese.

"Is that good?" I hear you ask.

Well, yes, it turns out manganese is handy for healthy bones, skin and blood sugar, as well as being an antioxidant (what isn't these days? OK, pork pies perhaps). Now, bear with me on this. The plot thickens.

When you Google "pineapple", you don't have to look far before you get onto pineapple throwing. Which in turn leads on to that singular human passion for throwing peculiar things. Wellies, cow pats, dwarves... they all come in for a bit of recreational launching, and that's just in England. Pineapple throwing is popular in Australia and has become an Australia Day tradition. Australia Day takes place on 26th January, which just happens to coincide with the festival of San Vicente de Martir in Spain – the one where they throw a goat off a tower.

How about that!

But the coincidence doesn't end there. The Spanish goat throwing fiesta (they're not allowed to use a real live goat any more, before you write in and complain) takes place in the town of, wait for it... Manganeses de la Polvarosa. Which very roughly translates as 'Explosive Manganeses'.

And that reminds me... you can eat too much pineapple.

Have a fruity weekend.

7

TRUMP

It's one of those words that gets sillier the more you say it. Trump. Trump. Trump. Trump. Trump. See what I mean? Trump. Try putting 'President' in front of it and it sounds even more ridiculous, doesn't it? But in case the ridiculous should become a reality, as it tends to do in matters of politics, it might help to understand a little more about the word Trump.

Trump.

You can bet he's had a team of branding specialists looking into the etymology of his name and this is what they would have unearthed. Firstly, the two chief meanings of trump: one being to overpower or outsmart, as in 'trump card', which he somehow managed to do to Ted Cruz this week; the other being to fabricate, as in 'trumped up', which… no, let's not go there. I seem to recall he has a team of ferocious lawyers too.

Interestingly, the two meanings have different roots but seem to have come together in one man. Trump as in 'trump card' is derived from the word 'triumph', whereas trump as in 'trumped up' stems from the French word 'tromper', meaning to deceive. Obvious really. There are also links to trumpets, fools, elephants etc etc.

So, all in all a perfect name for a Presidential candidate, you might think. But then there's the schoolboy definition, which I won't spell out here for the sake of delicacy, but might just prove to be the most apposite of them all.

Six months after writing this word, Donald Trump was elected President of the United States of America.

8

HEDONIC

I stumbled upon the word Hedonic this week while trying to read a scientific paper on drug abuse (well, you've got to kill the time between *Rip Off Britain* and *Homes Under the Hammer* somehow). I also stumbled (and I mean stumbled) upon 'neuropharmacology', 'extrapyramidal', and 'accumbens', at which point, I have to admit, I started skimming.

Hedonic is a great word, meaning 'relating to pleasure', from the Greek word 'hedone' (pleasure), and giving us the school of philosophy, Hedonism, which embraces the belief that life is for deriving maximum pleasure from everything you do. Well, who wouldn't embrace a philosophy like that!

Who said Plato?

No-one likes a smartarse. OK, apart from Plato, who wouldn't embrace a philosophy like that? As Woody Allen once said, "You can live to be a hundred if you give up all the things that make you want to live to be a hundred."

The thing about drugs and pleasure, so I've read, is that they don't actually give you pleasure, they only make you think they do by causing you pain and then giving you a smidgin of relief. It's like nicking the tiles off your roof and then selling them back to you.

So they're not really hedonic at all.

And if that's not enough to help you quit smoking this weekend, I give up.

9

SOCCER

Cup Final Day tomorrow, so this week we're talking spherical objects. Want to know how to wind up a British football fan? Well, there are many ways – in fact, if they're a Spurs fan the ways are almost too many to enumerate – but there is one surefire way to rile just about any British fan.

Open your mouth and utter the word 'soccer'. Then take cover. This exercise is not to be undertaken lightly.

You'll be surprised just how irate they get. 'Soccer', they'll tell you, is another one of those 'ugly Americanisms'. But, like so many people who rail against 'ugly Americanisms', they'll be wrong. 'Soccer' is as English as spotted dick.

Responsible Victorians in 1863, needing an abbreviation for their new form of entertainment, Association Football, to put up against Rugby Football's 'rugger', decided not to go with the more logical first choice but plumped instead for 'soccer'. And the rather strange name spread around the world.

It would be another 18 years before anyone referred to the game as simply 'football' and, even so, 'soccer' remained in popular usage for another hundred years. It was only in the 1980s, when Chris Waddle's haircut shocked everyone into a wholesale restructuring of the game, that 'soccer' fell out of favour in Britain. They kept using it in America, though, where the mullet was yet to be deemed a criminal offence, and hence the misconception that 'soccer' originated across the pond.

So enjoy the soccer tomorrow. May the boldest team win.

10

PORTMANTEAU

Chillax. Gaydar. Shopaholic. Pornucopia… yep, I finally made the scriptwriting team for *Made in Chelsea*. Actually, no. This week we're talking portmanteau words – words that combine the sound and meaning of two other words. They're all the rage these days, aren't they? Back in war time our forefathers were rationed to one – smog – but today it seems you can't come up with any new concept without someone trying to turn it into a portmanteau word.

Brexit, for example. Aaaaaaaaaaaaaaagh! I said it.

Brexit is a horrible portmanteau word and not just because it's become the most soul-destroyingly tedious debate in current affairs. It's a bad portmanteau word because there's no craft to it.

Lewis Carroll would turn in his grave, for it was he, one of the greatest of all wordsmiths, who first described such words as being like a portmanteau – a portmanteau being a type of suitcase formed of two compartments that close together. Humpty Dumpty was explaining to Alice how the words in *Jabberwocky* had been formed; words like 'slithy' (slimy and lithe) and 'frumious' (furious and fuming).

Notwithstanding the fact that this was an egg talking to a

girl on a mind-bending trip, Carroll was onto something. One of his portmanteau words, 'chortle' (chuckle and snort), has certainly stood the test of time.

A portmanteau word works when there's a natural blend between the two original words. 'Affluenza' (a malaise afflicting people who are too comfortably off) effortlessly merges the 'flu' sounds of 'affluence' and 'influenza'. 'Chugger', on the other hand, merely lops the 'm' off 'mugger' and replaces it with the 'ch' of 'charity'. It's not clever and it's not clear either. 'Chugger' could have a multitude of unsavoury meanings.

The dweebs who coined the word 'Brexit' will argue that it has evolved from 'Grexit', which combines one of the 'e's of 'Greek' with the 'e' of 'exit' (genius!), and that it's a valid development of the English language.

Crollocks!

Brexit is a drabomination, a politiful, snoreseating attempt at wordplay, and whatever the referendum on 23 June throws up, the best outcome will be that we don't have to hear it mentioned any more.

So much for that vain hope. The country voted for it and we've had to live with it every day since.

11

DERBY

Tomorrow is Derby Day. Why is it called Derby Day? Because it's the day they run the Derby. And why is the race called the Derby? Because it was conceived at a party hosted by Edward Smith-Stanley, the 12th Earl of Derby. Why was he called the 12th... OK, that's enough of that.

So far, so straightforward.

But is this sporting connection to Derby the reason why we use the term 'derby' in reference to other sporting contests? The answer is simple:

Maybe.

Some words defeat the etymologists and 'derby' is one of them. Consider this. As England emerged from the Dark Ages, a popular form of entertainment was marching mob-handed into the neighbouring village on Shrove Tuesday and starting a fight. These local brawls were hugely entertaining and drew large crowds but the casualty count started to get out of hand, so someone decide to calm things down by throwing an inflated pig's bladder into the fray (a trick they might want to consider in Croydon of a Saturday night).

So evolved the origins of both football and rugby. For

centuries, these anarchic ball games took place in and among villages throughout England on Shrove Tuesday, until someone invented the pancake and the whole thing fizzled out. With one notable exception: the Royal Shrovetide Football Match that still takes place each year in Ashbourne, Derbyshire (you see where this is going?).

The people of Ashbourne claim that it's this link to Derbyshire that gives us the word 'derby', specifically used for a local sporting contest. And if you've ever seen the people of Ashbourne in action, you wouldn't argue. You wouldn't ask, for instance, why we don't call it a 'local Ashbourne'.

You might, however, ask why, if 'derby' implies local, it is generally used with the word 'local' in front of it. 'The local derby between United and City.' At which point, whoever has the misfortune of sitting next to you will probably turn away and just watch the game. Or the race. Or whatever.

Some words are best just enjoyed – and derby is one of them. Let's face it, as long as Moonlight Magic romps home in first, who cares about etymology?

Moonlight Magic came last.

12

RANDOM

To choose this week's word I took any old book from my bookshelf, stuck in a pin and it landed on the word 'random'. Imagine the chances of that!

It was a book I turn to a lot when I'm writing – a dog-eared biography of the French philosophical author Albert Camus, which just happens to be the perfect thickness to fit under the leg of the table and stop it wobbling. Now that's what I call existentialism! The quote into which I stuck my pin was this:

"It is necessary to fall in love... if only to provide an alibi for all the random despair you are going to feel anyway."

It's all good, upbeat stuff with Camus. But compare that quote to this one from Thomas Moore, the Lord High Chancellor of England under Henry VIII, who refused to acknowledge Henry as the Church of England's Supreme Head and consequently lost his own. Prior to his beheading (always the best time to get your thoughts down), Moore wrote:

"This wretched brain gave way, and I became a wreck at random driven, without one glimpse of reason or heaven."

His use of the word 'random' gives a hint of its original

meaning, i.e. 'at great speed', from the old French 'randir' – 'to run fast'. This came to be associated with impetuosity, lack of thought and care – imagine a horse and carriage being driven too fast; or Wayne Rooney lunging into a tackle in the 89th minute when England are a goal down and he's missed a couple of sitters.

You get the picture.

In fairness to Wayne, the sense that the world is spinning too fast and you're always scrabbling for control is one that afflicts 99% of people on the planet*, and for which there are only two known cures: listen to Test Match Special or get a cat.

Or both.

Anyway, from this sense of headlong haphazardness evolved the modern sense of the word 'random' – 'without any specific aim or purpose'. In stark contrast to Moore's 'random', it's become trendy to apply the word to those eccentric people who move slowly through the world, occasionally saying things that make everyone else stop in their tracks, scratch their head and feel slightly uneasy. The 1%. In the past they would have been called philosophers. Today, they're just 'random'.

*Statistic made up at random but probably true.

13

STERLING

So now we know the effect of Europe on Sterling. What a shocker! We all knew there'd be pressure but did anyone envisage such a drastic collapse? And what about the future? What if the confidence doesn't return? Surely Uncle Roy won't pick him again.

Ho ho!

Hands up everyone who saw that coming. Yeah, all right, so it was about as subtle as one of Raheem's stepovers, but you have to admit, right now it's easy to get confused – especially if you happen to be travelling up the M9.

So why do we use this strange word 'sterling' when talking about the pound? As with so many things, I like to blame King Henry II (well, come on, all that business with Thomas à Becket…). It was during his reign that the silver used to make our pennies (a pound in weight of which made a pound in value) was reduced from 99.9% pure to 92.5%. The addition of other metals produced a harder, more resilient coin, which became known as 'sterling', for reasons that are uncertain. It could be something to do with stars or starlings or, dare I say it, Eastern Europeans.

From the coin came the term 'sterling silver' and the word

'sterling' itself, meaning 'first class', from the sense of being 'up to the test'. Pre Henry II, merchants in the habit of testing coinage by biting it would find their gnashers sank in quite easily, whereas the introduction of sterling silver brought about an accidental but welcome boom for the dentistry business.

So there you have it: Sterling – not as pure but more resilient. Hmm. I guess we'll find out just how resilient in due course. But rather than wait to see if the oldest currency in continuous use can bounce back, perhaps we should just cut our losses and replace it with the Rashford.

14

SOMME

The Somme is a pleasant river that runs through Picardy in northern France, 153 miles to the English Channel. It's name means tranquility. Given the weather we've been having, you wouldn't mind the chance to lie for a while by a tranquil French river, would you?

Just lie there and dream.

Dream perhaps of this day 100 years ago. You're 18 years old, one of six pals recruited from your home town in England, all hunkered down together in a soggy trench after a week of rain. The deafening artillery barrage that has been pounding the German lines for six days has finally ceased. Those poppy fields aren't looking quite so pretty now. And the bad news is that the silence means your cue is imminent.

At 7.30am a whistle blows, quickly followed by another and another, until the whistles are blowing all along the line. Hollow, mournful whistles. Your commanding officer puts his boot on the ladder, shouts a few words of encouragement, climbs a rung and falls back dead, a machine gun bullet through his forehead. He was 24.

You're next up the ladder. You don't know it now but your chances of making it through the day alive are roughly 5 in 6. Your chances of surviving unhurt are little more than 50:50. Nevertheless, duty compels you to climb the ladder, walk forward towards the barbed wire… and hope.

100 years ago today the British Army lost 19,240 men on the first day of the infantry battle on the Somme. It was the worst day of loss in British military history. The Germans lost between 10,000 and 12,000. All told, around 35,000 men were killed between dawn and dusk that day on that notorious battlefield – one death every one-and-a-quarter seconds.

The Somme is a pleasant river whose name means tranquility but it will forever be associated with that infamous day of carnage. And it didn't end there. The battle was allowed to rumble on for another 140 days, leaving more than a million killed or wounded.

Back home in England, the headmistress of Bournemouth High School for Girls assembled her sixth form and told them. "I have come to tell you a terrible fact. Only one out of 10 of you girls can ever hope to marry… It is a statistical fact. Nearly all the men who might have married you have been killed."

It's been a pretty disheartening week, what with one thing and another, and many miserable words have been exchanged, but this week's word stands as an eternal reminder of just how bad things can get.

"Somme," said one German soldier, reflecting on that battle. "The whole history of the world cannot contain a more ghastly word."

15

MAY

I may (or should that be 'might'?) be getting ahead of myself here, but if we're going to have to get used to hearing this word on an even more regular basis, we might (or should that be 'may'?) as well make sure we use it right.

(Or should that be 'correctly'?)

Funny little word, 'may'. A Yorkshire terrier of a word, it causes a lot more trouble than its size warrants. May has a multitude of meanings (ok, four meanings), all of them full of possibility, if somewhat tricky to define. There's the merry, merry month, which can either be the most delightful month of all – sunny, warm, verdant and brimming with all the fecund juiciness of spring – or a bitter winter hangover, its darling buds shaken by rough Shakespearean winds as the mercury barely dares to dabble in double figures.

But let's not talk about the weather. There's more to May than that. There's the 'let' meaning, as in 'May the best candidate win'. There's the 'can' meaning, as in 'May the last one out turn off the lights?'. And then there's the 'could' meaning, as in 'This may be the end of the world as we know it'. All good and simple.

But that's not actually the case, is it? If it was, we wouldn't use 'may' at all, we'd used 'let', 'can' and 'could' all the time. We don't because 'may', like so many words in the English language, has a subtle nuance that makes it the exact right word for certain situations. 'May the best team win' doesn't mean quite the same as 'let the best team win', does it? It means something more akin to 'Let the fates make it come to pass that the best team wins.' In other words, with May there's an implied sense of uncertainty.

Now there's a campaign slogan if ever I saw one.

16

GOLF

B ogey, birdie, dormie, caddie, niblick… If you like silly words (and let's be honest, who doesn't?), you'll find rich pickings around this time of the year when The Open golf tournament awakens from its annual slumber, opens one languid eye, swallows someone whole and nods off again.

Funny game, golf. Like Marmite, Brexit and heroin, you either adore it or revile it. There seem to be no half measures. But whichever camp you stand in, you have to admit it is a game resplendent with silliness and we should all be thankful for that. As Robert the Bruce once said while trying to smuggle his wife into the Members' Bar at Muirfield, "You can't blame the game for the social customs that surround it."

Golf has graced humanity with a unique platform for exercise, fun, social interaction, friendly competition, bitter rivalry, self-loathing and tormented introspection, sometimes all within the same shot. Were it not for the golden thread of silliness that binds it all together, golf would probably have destroyed us by now.

Why?

Because it's addictive, that's why. And it's addictive because it's difficult. Compared to other sporting skills, such as bowling a cricket ball, kicking a football or rolling a large cheese downhill, hitting a small ball with a thin slice of metal glued to the end of a long stick is about as challenging, skill wise, as anything the world of sport has ever come up with. Not surprisingly, it drives you mad. But get it right and you feel like a king. Or a queen. Just ask Mary Queen of Scots. One good chip on the 17th at St Andrews and she thought she was the Queen of England!

Mary was a big fan of golf and you'll often see her credited with having coined some of the game's colourful vocabulary. There's a grain of plausibility to this theory for two reasons:

1. She was Scottish.

2. She was French.

Two disparate cultures united by a common antipathy towards the English. Bring them together and strange and wonderful things occur – things like marmalade and the language of golf. 'Caddie' comes from the French 'cadet' (a young soldier), 'dormie' from the French 'dormir' (to sleep) and 'niblick' from the French 'n'oblique' (not shanked sideways into the thistles) – a definition which might very well have been made up.

Just now.

It's just struck me that if you have no interest in golf, this whole article so far will have read like a nonsense poem. But that's golf for you: sometimes it can leave you feeling like you've just gone 10 rounds with Hilaire Belloc. Yet it keeps you coming back for more because there's always that sense that gratification is just around the corner. As President Ford once said, "I know I'm getting better at golf because I'm hitting fewer spectators."

Fore!

17

CAMP

Woman goes to the doctor and says, "Doc, one minute I think I'm a wigwam, the next I think I'm a tipi." The doctor says, "You're too tense."

Yes, it's that time of year again. The season of the C word, time to drag out the canvas and corny jokes. Of course, 'camp' has two very different meanings. There's the Ranulph Fiennes sense and there's the complete polar opposite. Which is hard to define, given that Ranulph spends most of his time at one or other of the Poles, so as soon as you think you've discovered the polar opposite of Ranulph Fiennes it shifts to the other end of the Earth.

And here's an interesting fact for you: like fingerprints, eyeballs and snowflakes, no two tents are ever the same.

No really – I've researched it.

I discovered this while observing the accommodation at Latitude Festival last week, where all sorts of people could be seen grappling with all sorts of tents in all sorts of different and maddening ways. No-one could help anyone else because each tent presented its own unique challenge, and so the struggle went on in a frenzy of ferociously whippy poles and acres of fabric that could swallow a family of four for an entire weekend without anyone noticing. It was great spectator sport for someone like me, who discovered years ago that the best tent you can camp in is someone else's.

Once they'd eventually won their individual battles, the field was a mishmash of colourful and crazy geometrical shapes, showing all the design consistency of Croydon Town Planning Department. If there was a phrase that's the opposite of "If it ain't broke, don't fix it", it would have sprung to mind.

Despite the evident dissatisfaction with tent designs, 15 million Brits go camping and caravanning each year – a staggering statistic that can only be down to one thing: the rich vein of double entendres that camping throws up.

Just ponder that while you're grappling with your erection this summer.

18

SYNC

There comes a time in the lives of all men and women when we first hear the expression 'in sync' and our thoughts naturally fly to the washing up. Ah, the naivety of youth.

I still remember my first time. I had rushed out and bought *A Tonic For The Troops*, the new album from the Boomtown Rats (this was back in that narrow strip of history when people rushed out and bought albums by the Boomtown Rats) and I had settled in with my biscuit tins, Tupperware cake box and wooden spoons to listen to it five times through and drum along until I'd learnt it beat for beat and word for word.

What do you mean, 'weirdo'?

Anyway, one of the big hits off the album (hands up if you remember this) was *Like Clockwork*, which contained the line 'And we think in sync like clockwork'.

I can laugh about it now but when you don't know that 'sync' is a word but do know that 'sink' is a word, it's all very disconcerting. 'Think in sink'? Why would you get in a sink to think? Even if you are Bob Geldof? My daughter used to get in the sink but she was two years old. We'd just throw in the dishes and she'd have it all done in a couple of minutes. Teach em young, that's what I say.

But I digress. At the same time that the Rats were recording *A Tonic For The Troops*, a bloke called Chris Kelly was presenting a programme on ITV called *Clapperboard*. Remember it? *Clapperboard* was a half-hour film review programme for kids and it began with one of those iconic hinged slates that they use to start the shooting of a film scene.

OK, so I understood that this was called a clapperboard because it made a loud 'clap' sound, but what was the point of it, I wondered? A little investigation told me that it was all about the sync. The loud clap makes it easy for the film editor to line up the audio and video on the editing machine so that sound and image are in sync and not looking like a scene from *The Water Margin*.

Clever.

Interestingly, the abbreviation of synchronisation (try saying that with a mouthful of crackers) is as old as the film industry itself, although back in the 1920s they preferred the spelling 'synch'. This, however, became confused with the word 'cinch', which they needed for Broadway musicals, so they dropped the 'h' during the war – a good time to bury bad consonants. And drop Hs.

Thus I learnt what 'sync' means and I was able to sing along to *Like Clockwork* without even thinking about the washing up... that is until my mum told me to 'stop denting my biscuit tins' and come and do the washing up.

19

WASP

Wasp. Aargh! What is it good for? Absolutely n…

OK, I know the Olympics are kicking off and interest rates have been cut and there's still outrage over David Cameron's hamster being put forward for a peerage, but the big issue concerning me right now is a hole that's appeared in my back garden. Is it a sinkhole? Nope. A fox perhaps? No again. Badger then? Thrice no. This particular hole has been dug out by none other than a colony of wasps. How do I know? Because in the bottom of the hole, brazen as you like, I found a colony of wasps.

Absolutely bang to rights.

Back in April I wrote about bees, specifically bumble bees, and how they nest in the ground. This was not covered in *Winnie the Pooh*. If, like most right-thinking people, you lived by the lessons of AA Milne, you could quite easily drift through life assuming that bees make their hives exclusively in trees. So it came as a surprise to discover that they like to keep their feet on the ground. Now I discover that wasps do too.

Finding yourself standing over a hole full of wasps is no

laughing matter. You become acutely aware that it's a very short flight from hole in the ground to trouser leg and once a swarm of wasps goes up your trousers it's all over. So I backed away carefully and ran to look up 'wasps nest in ground'.

Of the search items that came up on page 1 of Google, four contained the words 'get rid', three contained 'removal' and two contained 'kill'. Why do we hate wasps so much? Change 'wasps' to 'bees' and you get just one 'get rid' and two 'removals'. The rest is all peace, love and happiness.

Yes, wasps sting. So do bees. Sure, they eat your picnic. So do cows. I didn't find a single website offering to 'get rid of cows' from my back garden. Ah, but bees make honey and cows make cheese. What are wasps good for?

Well, there are some things actually, like eating aphids and doing a spot of pollinating, but that's by the by. If we applied that reasoning to the human race there would be pages and pages of companies offering to get rid of Southern Rail, and then where would we be?

Not stuck on this sodding platform, that's for sure.

20

ZYXT

This bloke came up to me the other day and he said, a little smugly, "I've just finished reading the dictionary... "

"Wow!" I said. "Did you learn anything interesting?"

"Yes," he said. "The zebra did it."

I think he was trying to be funny but I wasn't having it. Being falsely accused of a crime is no laughing matter. Everybody knows the Zyzzyva did it.

What's a zyzzyva? It's a big-nosed weevil that lives in the American tropics and feeds on palm leaves, of course. More to the point, it's the last word in the dictionary. The American dictionary, that is. The *Oxford English Dictionary*, in its wisdom, refuses to recognise 'zyzzyva' (probably due to its criminal record) and leaves us instead with the word 'zyxt'.

Like oast houses, Gypsy Tarts and the White Cliffs of Dover, 'zyxt' is a Kentish creation, a now obsolete word that was once used by Kentishmen, or men of Kent, or possibly neither, to mean 'you see'. As in "Zyxt that small, rotten apple? That's your dinner, that is." Or, "Listen you yaugh yawnup, touch my zoster and I'll give you a good bannicking, zyxt!" Why it fell out of use is beyond me, but if you're planning an expedition to Kent and you want some words to help you get by, you'll find some beauties in this Dictionary of the Kentish Dialect[3].

Of course, it wasn't so long ago that z wasn't the last letter in the alphabet. As any 19th century schoolchild will tell you, the alphabet used to end with the 'and' symbol &, now known as 'ampersand'. When reciting the alphabet, those 19th century schoolchildren would follow any letter that formed a word in its own right, e.g. A or I, with the Latin 'per se' (by itself) and then the letter again.

Zyxt?

So when they came to &, they would say, "And per se and," which became contracted to "ampersand". Try it for yourself.

So anyway, I went back to that bloke and said, a little smugly, "Actually, I think you'll find the ampersand did it." He had no answer to that.

21

DAREDEVIL

Ever since Perseus went and lopped the head off Medusa, there have been elements of the human race who have been prepared to do anything to avoid the quiet life – people who could only enjoy life, in fact, by getting as close as possible to death without quite shuffling off this mortal coil.

Back in April an escapologist from Yorkshire called Antony Britton nearly pegged out trying to succeed where Harry Houdini had failed a century earlier, by escaping from a grave filled with earth. Had he watched this video[4] he might have thought twice. It's a magnificent Pathe newsreel showing the magician Alan Alan trying the same stunt in 1949, equipped only with a length of string, some cardboard and a pair of swimming trunks.

He failed.

Don't worry, he lived to tell the tale. Until 2014, in fact. If you didn't have the commentary, you might think Alan Alan was being subjected to a particularly sadistic form of torture. But no, Alan Alan was entirely compliant in the stunt because Alan Alan was a daredevil.

The first recorded use of the word 'daredevil' dates back to the late 18th century (a century before the word 'adrenaline'), around the time when eccentric Continentals were going up and down in winged balloons for the delight of the fee paying public. The word was formed from two other words, 'dare' and – you guessed it – 'devil'. Ah, but to whom did the word 'devil' refer? Was it the bloke going up and down in the balloon – i.e. a devil of daring – or the Devil himself – was the balloonist daring the Devil, as a killjoy kills joy?

It doesn't matter, does it? The word may have been new but the daredevil wasn't. Even by the late 1700s, men and women had been sticking feathers to their arms and jumping off towers for the best part of a thousand years, all to escape the mundanity of the daily grind.

The age of motorised transport presented the daredevil with all sorts of new possibilities, from walking up and down the roof of steaming trains to riding motorbikes around vertical walls or leaping over canyons. But amidst all that high-speed heroism, there was still something more captivating about an old woman floating over Niagara Falls in a barrel or a Frenchman dancing between the Twin Towers on a rope.

Because the beauty of becoming a daredevil is that you don't need much in the way of equipment. Why go to the expense of taking a balloon into space, for example, when you can keep your feet on the ground and stick your head in the jaws of a lion?

So if you've spent the last couple of weeks being made to feel inadequate by all those Olympians in Rio and you've vowed to push yourself a bit harder this weekend, get yourself a small canon and a crash helmet and immortality could be yours.

Until it all goes wrong, of course.

22

PRUNE

Anyone who's been subjected to this Word of the Week lark from day one will remember that "prune" is what Victorians used to say in order to pull the appropriate face when being photographed. That was before the wanton "cheese" took over and the whole fabric of polite society began to fall apart.

A fine, upstanding word, prune. It has three very diverse meanings: first up, the dried plum, *Prunus domestica*, that you eat at your own risk; secondly, an insulting term for someone who sours the occasion – a sourpuss, a party pooper, a git; and thirdly, the verb to reduce by removing elements, normally applied to trees and shrubs.

By the way, if you haven't summer pruned your fruit trees yet, now is the time.

And if you need advice, call an arborist. Arborists are experts in all things trees. The Arboricultural Association has one of the great URLs: Trees.org.uk. It does exactly what it says on the trunk. Arborists are not tree huggers, they are tree consultants and they carry an incredible amount of power. Why? Because even in these days of powerful multinational corporations riding roughshod over the land, anything of natural importance like a tree, a newt or a butterfly can still bring the bulldozers to a grinding halt.

Kinda reassuring, isn't it?

It doesn't matter how many zillions you turn over or how many farmers you put out of business each year, if there's a tree standing in the way of your new hypermarket and an arborist deems it to be of importance, you have to find some other bit of landscape to blot.

Entomologists carry similar clout. You might not think so to look at them but, as Shakespeare might have said if he'd worked for Tesco, "the butterfly net is mightier than the gun". Enterologists, on the other hand, have less influence when it comes to building on the Green Belt. They tend to be more concerned with prune encounters of the first kind.

23

SPELUNKING

What's the first thing that enters your head when you see this word? No, on second thoughts, don't tell me. Unless, of course, the first thing that entered your head was the Latin word 'spelunca' and you immediately deduced that spelunking must have something to do with caves.

Hands up everyone who did Latin at school. I did. Not very well, mind you. My crowning glory was waking up mid-lesson and launching into a translation of some text about spears and caves before realising that everyone was looking at me not in admiration but amusement, because the teacher hadn't asked me to translate at all, I'd merely dreamed he had.

My first introduction to Latin was some smart-arse at primary school who had learnt from his brother how to sing *I Love You Love* by Gary Glitter in the old language. (This was the early 70s.) 'Amo amas, amas amare...' Jeez, the things that stick in your mind. Brrrrrrrwgh.

They say Latin is a dead language. For me it went beyond death. In fact, there are parts of my brain that are still resurrecting. But one thing I do remember is that 'spelunca' means (or meant) cave. I've forgotten the word for spear – perhaps one of you can enlighten me – but spears and caves seemed to feature in just about every piece of Latin text I ever saw. Strange really. I thought the Romans were more sophisticated than that. Where were all the texts about wine and aqueducts and orgies?

'Spelunca' sticks in the mind because it's a beautifully euphonious word, as is its derivative 'spelunking', which, by the way, means 'the exploration of caves'.

A bit disappointing really. You want it to be more onomatopoeic than that, don't you? I've not done a lot of cave exploring, on account of the fact that it seems silly to put yourself under tons of earth until you really have to, but I'm pretty sure that the sound cave explorers make is nothing like 'spelunking' – unless they fall into a sump and dink their melon on a stalagmite on the way in.

24

CLICHÉ

I came within a whisker of making 'bun' the Word of the Week, following a thought-provoking discussion over a Danish pastry (life is never dull). I was, quite rightly in my opinion, reprimanded for referring to said pastry as a 'bun' and it struck me as interesting that I should misuse a word like that.

But, on reflection, not that interesting.

So I stuck to plan A and plumped for 'cliché'. Now, pay attention because there'll be a test at the end of this article. Cliché is an interesting word and here's why. Just about everyone knows that clichés are bad and should be avoided at all costs (and if you don't know, there'll always be a self-righteous writer close at hand to tell you so), yet just about everyone uses clichés on a regular basis (including those self-righteous writers).

That's how they become clichés in the first place. It's a Catch-22.

Cliché was originally a French printing term. Back in the 19th century, print type was set in a solid plate called a stereotype, 'stereo' coming from the Greek meaning 'solid'. The 'stereo' in your sound system doesn't mean 'two', it refers to the solid, 3D effect of the sound, not the fact that it comes through two separate channels as opposed to one (mono). I'm going off at a tangent now.

So, getting back to the point, French printers called their stereotype a 'cliché' – possibly because of the sound it made, possibly just because they were French – and hence, 'cliché' came to be used for a phrase or saying that has become set in stone. Any expression that gets used a lot is, by definition, a cliché, which is where the problem lies, because it's generally the best, most inventive expressions that get used the most.

So why is it wrong to use clichés? There's the rub. The simple answer is that it shows a lack of original thought. On the flipside of the coin, clichés can help to cut to the chase because their meaning is clear as day. 'Singing from the same hymn sheet', for example, is very evocative and gets its message across succinctly. But don't go there on pain of death, unless you're wearing an ironic bow tie and big glasses, in which case it's expected of you.

The challenge for the humans among us is to strive constantly for new ways of saying things. And sorry, misquoting your clichés doesn't count. 'Step foot'? 'Heart wrenching'? 'Damp squid'? Don't be silly. The bottom line is that the sparkling stream that is the English language becomes stagnant and sickly if we all keep using the same clichés. Shakespeare didn't use clichés, he originated them. End of argument.

So, how many clichés can you count in this article?

First correct answer wins a bun.

25

WEEVIL

How much do you know about weevils? "How much do I want to know?" I hear you cry. OK, fair point. But wait. What if I told you that the weevils you think of when you think of weevils weren't weevils at all? And the weevils that are weevils gave us Muddy Waters, Smokey Robinson and Diana Ross?

Hah! Not so dismissive now.

The weevils you think of when you think of weevils are, of course, the ones that stowed away on Walter Raleigh's ships and provided the nourishment in his biscuits. Also known as bread beetles or, due to their fondness for pharmaceuticals, drugstore beetles, these little critters are, as those alternative names suggest, beetles. Not weevils.

In fact, so often are they wrongly referred to as weevils that people who care actually refer to them as 'non-weevils'. That's a bit like referring to a human as a 'non-horse', although, to be fair, humans don't generally get confused with horses – well, certain members of the Royal Family aside.

Better still, weevils that really are weevils are referred to as 'true weevils' – one of the great unmade film titles if ever there was one. Sequels include *Resident Weevil* and *The Weevil Dead*.

One of the things that distinguish a weevil from a non-weevil is its long snout, which it uses for boring into plants, often with devastating effect. The boll weevil, for example, laid waste to the cotton crop throughout the American south in the early 20th century and thus triggered the Great Migration that gave us jazz, blues, Motown and every other cultural nugget that has come out of the Mississippi Delta, Chicago, Detroit etc, not to mention the peanut industry, which thrived in the Deep South as farmers were forced to diversify away from cotton, and Delta Airlines, which grew from a crop dusting operation specifically targeted at the boll weevil.

If you could have a conversation with a boll weevil, it would probably claim a hand in the Civil Rights movement too, and it would be hard to argue against it. Funny how something so small can have such a profound influence on the history of humankind. The boll weevil originally crossed over into Texas from Mexico. If only someone had thought to build a wall.

26

FROCK

Contrary to the rumours, I'm not really interested in frocks. Women's fashion is baffling enough without trying to understand the difference between a frock and a dress – if indeed there is any difference – or why nobody seems to be able to use the word without an ironic smirk.

No, what interests me more is the antonym 'defrock', which is what happens to priests when they've been bad. In fact, 'defrock' is not an antonym of 'frock' because one is a verb and the other is a noun. There is no verb 'to frock'. So how do you get 'defrocked'?

It conjures visions of priests being caught wearing dresses and having them ripped off by a delegation from the Vatican, which I'm sure doesn't happen any more. (Does anyone else have these visions, by the way, or is it only me?) But that's the problem that can arise when a word goes through several changes of meaning. We might know a frock today as a light, loose fitting dress of the sort that a young girl might wear to the seaside, but in the 14th century it meant a monk's habit and came to be used for the loose cloak worn by a priest.

Hence, defrocking being the removal of the trappings and rights of priesthood. It all makes sense when you look into it. It's just not as funny as the idea of a priest in a dress.

All that apart, it has to be said that 'frock' is a more interesting word than 'dress' and the beauty of the English language is that it gives us these alternatives to use whenever we want to liven things up a bit. Dorothy Parker liked to liven things up. This is the literary genius responsible for such witticisms as,

"If all the girls who attended the Yale prom were laid end to end, I wouldn't be a bit surprised."

And,

"Brevity is the soul of lingerie."

In her poem *Faute de Mieux* (meaning For Want of a Better Alternative), she chose 'frock' over 'dress':

Travel, trouble, music, art,
A kiss, a frock, a rhyme
I never said they feed my heart,
But still they pass my time.

And that's good enough for me.

27

PANTS

O K, I'll keep this brief…

Ah, please yourselves. Let's play a little word association game. If I say to you 'Sam Allardyce', what's the first word that pops into your mind?

Hands up everyone who said 'pants'.

QED. A disgruntled Alan Shearer (is there any other kind of Alan Shearer?) used words like 'catastrophic', 'incredible', 'misjudgement', 'laughing stock' and 'get'. He could have saved himself a lot of trouble and just said 'pants'. The great thing about 'pants' with reference to the short-lived erstwhile England manager is that it could be both something he does and something he is.

Clever thing, language.

Pants is a word that could have been invented to describe England managers but, of course, it wasn't. It wasn't invented to describe pants either – not pants as we know them. The word is derived, as we all know, from the French 'pantalons', which today means trousers but originally referred to a more skinny garment like tights, as favoured by court jesters, fools and the like. (Hands up everyone who's thinking 'Allardyce'). This became 'pantaloons' in English, which was abbreviated to 'pants' in the late 1800s.

It's easy to forget that the British 'pants' is an abbreviation of 'underpants' and, therefore, the bit we've kept actually refers not to the undergarment but to the outer garment that we criticise the Americans for calling 'pants'. But who cares? Our pants are funnier than their pants and that's all that matters.

'Pants' has been in common usage as a derogatory term since at least, well, since I tried to nutmeg Matt N at football training and he looked at me disdainfully and said, 'That was pants.' In that moment I knew my vocabulary had been gifted a gem that would light up the remainder of my life. I've used the word countless times since and intend to keep doing so to the end. Indeed, I can't think of a more fitting last word.

'Pants...'

That first encounter with the adjectival 'pants' must have been around the turn of the millennium, yet the dictionaries are still only grudgingly acknowledging the definition of 'pants' as anything other than a garment or something a dog or an England manager does. This is because most dictionaries are American and they haven't been blessed with 'pants' as an adjective. Why would they? There's nothing funny about comparing something to a pair of trousers.

28

THAT

N o, my expletive loving friends, that's not a typo, though it might well be, as I will explain. This week I really am taking up your valuable bandwidth with a few comments on that unassuming little pronoun/adverb/determiner/conjunction that is 'that'.

In over three decades of writing and editing for a living, I've come across a lot of typos. One million, two hundred and forty three thousand, six hundred and twenty tow – make that twenty three – at the last count. Of all those many typos, one recurs more than any other. See if you can guess what it is.

No, not 'broccoli'. Not 'Morocco' either. Not even 'separate', 'accommodate' or 'gauge'. The word that gets misspelt more than any other is 'that'.

"What? How? Why?" you're probably thinking. How can anyone misspell a word as simple as 'that'? In fact, it's not a case of misspelling 'that' in the sense of being unable to spell it, but in the sense of spelling it when you should be spelling something else – specifically 'than'.

Comparative phrases such as 'more than', 'rather than' etc become 'more that', 'rather that' and so on. Why? I'll tell you why.

It's all to do with a small wiring fault that occurs in an area of the brain known as the Conjunctive Nebula, which lies somewhere between the Cerebral Aurora and Shatner's Bassoon. While your mind puts together a sentence such as, "You are older than me," this glitch causes you to write, "You are older that me."

Watch out for it. You'll start seeing it everywhere.

Apart from here, of course.

29

TRILLION

I talk to the trees but they don't listen to me." So sang Clint Eastwood in *Paint Your Wagon*. It was the song that both began and ended his singing career, an optimistic little love song that briefly offered a tantalising glimpse into the soul of the Pale Rider before slamming the window shut again.

Recent revelations suggest that those opening lyrics were, however, not entirely accurate. It's not that the trees weren't listening, more a case of selective deafness. Thanks to not at all eccentric German woodland expert Peter Wohlleben, we now know that trees do talk, to each other at least. They also nurture their young, warn one another of danger and show fear.

Wer wußte!

Anyway, it's when you delve deeper into such stories that you come across amazing stats like this: there are an estimated 3,040,000,000,000 trees on planet Earth. Three trillion and a bit, in other words (even if that 'bit' does happen to be 40 billion.) It's all relative.

Trillion is not a word you often hear bandied about. Not even Brian Cox uses it, preferring the more scientific "billions and billions". In fact, you could be forgiven for thinking it's a word invented solely to describe the national debt.

But it's not. The word 'trillion' was, as the name suggests, invented to describe a million to the power of three: a million, million, million. Back then a billion meant a million million. You can see the logic.

So where did the logic go?

I seem to be forever defending the Americans against false accusations of taking literal liberties but I have to do so again, for it was the Italians and French, not the Americans, who changed the definition of 'trillion' to a million million and 'billion' to a thousand million. Something to do with a change in the way big numbers were written – grouping the zeros into threes rather than sixes. Not much of an excuse, if you ask me.

And it's not a recent development either. Though it took Britain until the 1970s to capitulate and fall into line, the original 'long scale' trillion was a 15th century invention and the change in magnitude to the 'short scale' took place in the late 17th century. You wonder what they had in sufficient quantities to merit inventing such a vast number in the first place.

Trees I suppose.

And stars.

30

GAGE

Those of you who were paying attention two weeks ago will recall that I was banging on about words that are commonly misspelt ('that' being the chief example), and I happened to allude to 'gauge' as one of those words that often trips people up. That pesky 'u' just never seems to sit in the right place, does it?

So this week I've taken the easy way out and plumped for a form of gage that doesn't bother with such things as silent 'u's. I'm talking, of course, about the word 'gage'.

I was chatting to a solicitor friend of mine (I like to drop that in from time to time just to keep my enemies on their toes) and he suggested that I make 'mortgage' the Word of the Week, racy little devil that he is. He then proceeded to expound his theory on the origins of the word 'mortgage' and the conversation took an instant turn for the intriguing.

The 'mort' bit is obviously from the French for 'dead', as in 'mortal' (subject to death), 'mortician' (someone who works with the dead, not to be confused with 'Mourinho', which currently has a similar meaning), and 'Morden' (where tube trains go to die). The 'gage' bit was altogether more obscure.

To shine the necessary light onto this old word, we have to

take ourselves back, once again, to the Middle Ages (blimey, we might as well buy a house there!), when England was a land ravaged by fragrant French nobles with a strong sense of chivalry and a taste for the histrionic. For them the glove or gauntlet was symbolic of a pledge. If you wanted to promise a fellow noble that you could be trusted to escort their wife to Dover without trying to pick the lock of her chastity belt, you would remove your glove, fold it and hand it to him. This was known as a 'gage' and the word was used, incidentally, as an alternative to the Old English 'wed', from which we get 'wedding'. It's why you get 'engaged' to be married. Or become 'engaged' in battle.

Or both at the same time, in some cases.

For the 'gage' was also used as a symbol of a challenge, and evolved into the word 'wage', which explains the link between waging war and picking up your wages. The aggressor would, quite literally, throw down the gauntlet and the recipient would, just as literally, take it up. That's assuming they wanted to accept the challenge. If they didn't fancy it they could just cock their nose in the air, mutter "Nah, je ne le fanci pas," turn on their heel and flounce off to hold their manhoods cheap.

So a mortgage was a 'dead pledge', which suggests you were expected to either pay your instalments on time or die. In fact, it wasn't quite as intimidating as modern mortgage lenders would have it. The 'dead' bit actually referred to the fact that the pledge died on repayment, or on repossession of the property. All a bit disappointing really.

But not half as disappointing as the origin of the name 'greengage', which has nothing at all to do with chain mail gloves or French duellists. The plum-like fruit is called a greengage because it's green and it was introduced to England by a bloke called Gage. Nothing more romantic than that, I'm afraid.

That said, the French name for it is 'Reine Claude', in honour of the 16th century Duchess of Brittany, who became the Queen Consort of King Francis I of France after a particularly choppy crossing from Dover.

31

FAUCET

There are many words you could use to describe the American Presidential election. You'll have your own favourites. The word that kept popping into my mind was 'faucet'. This is probably why international TV crews no longer come to me for comment on such occasions.

I bought a faucet this week, although I had to use the word 'stopcock' to avoid annoying the bloke in Plumbwell. Fine word though 'faucet' is, we just don't get to use it in Britain and I think that's a shame.

Regular readers have probably grown tired of my insistence on defending America against accusations of misuse of the English language, especially in such a week as this, but as a lifelong defender of Truth, Justice and the Purley Way, I feel it's important to set the record straight.

And not just because my son banned me from laying 'PATRONIZE' in Scrabble last night. Bless him.

"Schvymxckzuh," I said, "why is Scrabble so important to you?" He simply told me American spellings weren't allowed. I had to hold back from delivering a two-hour lecture on the words that we regard as American but actually aren't.

Words like 'faucet'.

A faucet is a tap, originally a tap for extracting the booze from a barrel – the best kind of tap – but nowadays a tap that delivers American water through American pipes. (How it ever became known as a 'cock' is a whole other story). It's a word we don't use in English – but we did, long ago.

And the same goes for many other 'Americanisms'. Garbage. Apartment. Broiler. Vacation. Diaper. Candy. Patronize… Like faucet, these aren't words the Americans have invented just to be different, they're words they've hung on to while we've moved on. So who are the upstarts with no respect for their roots?

What you have to understand about America is that, for all its space missions and silicon and special sauce, significant swathes of the country are quaintly old-fashioned. There's a town in Nebraska, for example, where they still eat with a knife and fork. Many of the nation's customs were established by the religious refugees and fur trappers who colonised the place centuries ago and much of their language is left over from their English forefathers.

If you want to trace these things all the way back to their source, you'll find that the use of 'ize' predates 'ise' in English because it comes from the Greek verb endings 'izo' and 'izein'. "H to the izo, V to the izein," as Jay-Z might have sung had he been an entertainer in the court of Theseus. Of course, he wasn't.

The more widespread use of 'ise' in Britain probably evolved to avoid confusion with words like 'revise', 'surprise' and 'exercise' that never took the 'ize' ending in the first place because they derived from non-Greek origins. So it was we Brits who waived the rules.

Oxford Dictionaries, the ultimate authority on the use of English after my Dad, concludes: "In British English, it doesn't matter which spelling convention is chosen: neither is right or wrong, and neither is 'more right' than the other."

So what's my point? 112 points, that's my bleedin' point! On a triple word score with a 50 point bonus? Come on!

32

TENDER

Here's a word that will trigger very different responses in readers, depending on whether you work in a bank, a hospital, in new business development, on the railways, at sea, or, like me, you just walked into the corner of a particularly unyielding worktop.

It reminds me of the time I got hit in the thigh by a hockey ball and a bruise came up that looked like an Indian sunset. Beautiful thing it was, all the colours of the rainbow. I had coach loads of hippies beating a path to my door just to sit and gaze at it. "How does it feel?" they would ask. "Tender," I'd say. There was no better word. I couldn't so much as tickle it without letting out an involuntary honk, like a donkey backing onto a cactus.

So that was 'tender' in the 'soft and sensitive' sense of the word. But in any given week you might come across 'tender' in the form of 'a nurse', 'currency', 'a formal offer or bid', 'the wagon that carries coal behind a steam train', or 'one of those little boats that are attached to the back of big boats'. Not necessarily in that order.

"How on earth do things like this happen?" you may well wonder. Here's the recipe. Take a bunch of Latin words, force them through a medieval French sieve, catapult them into England, muddle with a flagon of mead and leave to simmer with the lid off for a couple of centuries. In this case, the raw Latin ingredients were the adjective 'tenerem', meaning 'delicate or youthful', the verb, 'tendere', meaning 'to extend', and the extension of that, 'attendere', meaning 'to attend to' (literally 'extending' your attention to). The first two became 'tendre' in French and then 'tender' in English. The third became 'attendre' in French and 'atenden' in English, which was pared down over a gentle heat to 'tend'. And thus the nurse became the 'tender'.

I'll give you a moment to digest that.

Right, onwards. This same derivation gave us the train bit and the boat bit, since both 'attend' to the mothership, so to speak. The 'extend' meaning gave us the formal offer, since you extend an offer, and that in turn gave us the currency, since you offer currency.

It's important to understand all this so you don't make the mistake of trying to commission F Scott Fitzgerald to write your bid documents, or thinking Elvis went around singing songs of devotion to the back end of locomotives. I'm not saying he didn't – what Elvis did in his spare time was Elvis' business, as far as I'm concerned – but I can state with complete confidence that *Love Me Tender* was not about a coal wagon.

Right, where's the Arnica?

33

PITH

Tis the season of the satsuma, that Christmassy citrus delight that's so easy to peel and fills the room with what 5th-century Chinese poet Liu Hsun described as a "fragrant mist". Not to be confused with the "fragrant mist" used by 20th century poets to describe the urinals at Tottenham Court Road, this is the one that makes people stop work, sniff the aromatic air and exclaim, "Oi, who's eating an orange?"

You could argue that satsuma season always comes too late, following hard, as it does, on influenza season, when 90 per cent of the population get struck down by those battalions of bacteria that spend the summer months lying low under sun loungers and parasols, plotting their next epidemic. Just as we're recovering from the first wave of streaming eyes and hacking coughs and long, shivery nights longing for death to take us before the sun rises to sentence us to another day of suffering, along comes the satsuma like a gigantic vitamin C shaped bolt being drawn across the door of the empty stable.

Still, they're fun to eat and they're good for filling the toe end of a Christmas stocking. But I'm not here to talk satsumas, I'm here to talk pith.

Not for the firtht time, I hear you cry.

Very funny. Now pay attention. Slaughtermen and matadors will tell you that 'pith' is a verb meaning to kill an animal by severing its spinal column. But the slaughter of helpless animals is no subject for discussing at Christmas, so let's move swiftly on.

The pith we all know and love is, of course, the fibrous white stuff that clings to your satsuma after you've peeled it. There are few more satisfying things in life than removing the skin from a satsuma in one piece, but one of them is peeling the pith off afterwards. In fact, it's so fulfilling that it's sometimes used in prisons for pacifying uppity lifers. Instead of powerful sedatives, they're given several dozen satsumas to de-pith, after which they're rendered so docile that they're ready to step back into society and take up senior positions on the International Olympic Committee.

And then there's the pith helmet, that 19th century icon of the British Empire, not made from the pith of the satsuma but from the pith of the sola plant, which grows in Indian swamps. The pith helmet was adopted by the British military in tropical climes because it was light and offered protection from the sun. Its resistance to a bullet or spear was less impressive, however, and it also tended to present a prominent target for the enemy, poking up out of the long grass like a coconut asking to be shied. Realising this, soldiers took to dying the cloth covering of their helmets with tea and so devised the concept of camouflage. The garish scarlet jacket completed the look.

The distinctive shape of the pith helmet is thought to have been modelled on the German pickelhaube, the headgear favoured by kaisers and barons, made, as the name suggests, from the hollowed out husk of a giant gherkin. Actually, that's not true. The pickel bit was the spike stuck on top, which served as a useful place to keep your satsuma during hand-to-hand combat.

Kaiser Wilhelm, the doyen of the pickelhaube, was a pithy man. He said things like, "We will frighten the British flag off the face of the waters..." and "Give me a woman who really likes beer and I will conquer the world." Nobody was ever sure what he meant but he was terse, punchy and he didn't waste words.

We should all strive for pithiness in our communications – it's just the provocation of all out world war that we should seek to avoid.

34

BARGAIN

B lack Friday, Cyber Monday… it's all a bit Star Wars, isn't it? What will they come up with next, Wookiee Wednesday? So I refused to get drawn in this year, preferring to spend over the odds on my Christmas presents. I'm no fool.

My more pressing concern was laying my hands on an Advent calendar on the 1st December. Don't you find that Advent can creep up on you and take you by surprise? Someone should come up with a countdown of some kind so we can all see it coming in good time.

Anyway, I assumed that my favourite supermarket would have a bargain bin full of them, or that there would be a stack of them on that 'discounted items' shelf where they put the buns that are about to go stale and the unusual women's toiletries and the tins of chopped carrots and peas that even the harvest festival brigade rejected.

But no. I'd barely got the word 'Advent' out when I was greeted with nothing more than a sympathetic shrug from a woman who looked like she'd been employed specifically to give sympathetic shrugs to people asking for Advent calendars. She did it very well, I have to say. So this year the kids are going to have to cope with the run-up to Christmas with nothing to help them through but the thrill of anticipation and the spirit of goodwill. Tricky, I know, but when I was a child, Advent calendars had nothing behind the doors but a picture of a manger or a donkey or something, and that was more than enough to keep the excitement at boiling point for the full 24 days.

Different times.

So while I was quite pleased not to be force feeding chocolate to my progeny according to a prescribed timetable, my supermarket knock-back did send me into a bit of a trance and I left the shop with the word 'bargain' spiralling round the inside of my head. So fixated did I become with the word that I nearly forgot the cat food.

Do you ever get that with words, where the more you say them the more unfamiliar they sound until you become almost hypnotised by them? No? Well, I do so I'll carry on. And what obsessed me about 'bargain' was the way we pronounce it. What other words ending in 'ain' do we pronounce 'in'? OK, apart from 'captain'. And 'mountain'. Yes alright, and 'chaplain'.

In return I offer you 'plain', 'gain', 'grain', 'pain', 'Spain', 'train'. And it's not just the monosyllabic words: 'terrain', 'contain', 'explain', 'disdain', 'sustain', 'porcelain'... I rest my case.

There is no logical explanation for why we pronounce these words differently, any more than there is for a supermarket that turns nearly 9,000 tons of surplus food into animal feed every year not having a surplus Advent calendar on the first day of Advent. I mean, one measley Advent calendar!

Still, at least I got the word 'bargain' out of my head.

35

DERRICK

B atey, Nimmo, Guyler, Griffiths, Hatton, Jarman, Jacobi... If your name happens to be Derek, you have a statistically higher chance of becoming famous than if you're called Gilbert. And that's a fact.

O'Sullivan, Scott-Heron... See?*

The history of entertainment is liberally sprinkled with great Dereks. In addition to all the real ones there are the fictional ones like Derek Smalls, the self-proclaimed "lukewarm water" between the fire and ice of Spinal Tap, and Dudley Moore's Derek, oppo to Peter Cook's Clive, whose body of work represents a masterclass in the art of profanity and will become, like the Lead Codices of Jordan, the ultimate handbook for understanding this particular field of the English language. Sadly, having scoured Derek's entire panoply of famous quotes, I've failed to find any that I can reproduce in the sort of polite company we keep here.

Anyway, the point that emerges from all this with abundant clarity is that Derek the name is spelt D-E-R-E-K. Or at least I thought it was, until I googled 'famous Dereks' (don't you just love the fact that someone has actually created that website?) and discovered a smattering of blokes – mostly American footballers and basketball players – who called themselves D-E-R-R-I-C-K.

To any right-thinking individual, a derrick is one of those rickety looking towers they use for extracting oil from the ground. But the discovery of all these blokes being named after an oil pump called for further investigation, so I rolled my sleeves up, donned my hardhat and went to work. It turns out the derrick that does the oil digging took its name from an earlier definition – a crane with a pivoted arm. And it took that meaning from the hangman's gallows, which became known as a derrick in the 17th century. You can see the evolution. But here's the explosive bit. Why was the gallows called a derrick? After famous Elizabethan hangman Thomas Derrick.

So, annoyingly, it turns out I was wrong and Derrick is a bona fide name after all, albeit a surname. It is derived from the same German root as 'Dietrich', as in Marlene, which means 'ruler of folk'.

Derrick the 'killer of folk' was an interesting character – if 'interesting' is an apt description for a rapist who executed over 3,000 people. Alas, time turns monsters into legends. Derrick was forced to become a hangman by Robert Devereaux, 2nd Earl of Essex, in return for his pardon for the aforementioned rape, but he took to the task with inhuman zeal. Not content with stringing up his victims one by one with a rope slung over a wooden gibbet, he invented his own, more efficient contraption, using ropes and pulleys and a longer wooden arm, with which he could despatch them 23 at a time. The judges at Tyburn couldn't convict 'em fast enough.

In a particularly macabre twist of fate, Derrick even sent his pardoner, the Earl of Essex, to meet his maker after the Earl staged an ill-conceived coup d'état and was convicted of treason. The moral of which is, I suppose, be careful who you pardon.

If you can think of any other famous Gilberts, we'd love to hear them.

36

FORGETFULNESS

Now, what was I going to write about this week?

...

Nope, it's gone.

I had considered a piece on words that sound like two or more other words: words such as 'faucet', 'moron' and 'Israelites'. Words like these are among the great gifts of the English language, manna from Heaven for crossword compilers and people who like to misinterpret song lyrics. Remember that brilliant Maxell ad of the 1980s featuring the Desmond Dekker classic?

'Oh-oh me ears are alight.'

A frequent cry in my house is, 'Anyone seen my khaki?' If we were living in Utah this might be confusing but Reigate doesn't have a very large contingent of survivalists (or preppers as they quaintly call themselves), so whenever I hear that cry I know immediately that they're not referring to battledress but to the small metal object that unlocks the car. Or it would, if only we could find the bloody thing.

As an interesting aside, did you know that Utah is thinking of changing its nickname to The Condiment State? Because it's full of salt and preppers.

No? Please yourselves.

Forgetting where you left the car keys is such a common and specific affliction that you would think there'd be a proper medical name for it, wouldn't you? Despite an extensive internet search, however, the only term I could find was 'dementia', which I think is possibly overstating the point, especially as research has shown that people aged 18-34 forget where they put their car keys more often than over-55s do.

They're also twice as likely to forget what day of the week it is! According to the same survey, 15% of people aged 18-34 in the United States can't remember this simple detail. That's roughly one in seven, which, as any statistician will confirm, means that between them they are 100 per cent likely to forget the entire week!

The survey concludes with the revelation that two fifths of the American public have mislaid at least one everyday item in the past week – not entirely surprising, given that half of them lost their marbles last month*.

The paradoxical thing about 'forgetfulness' is that it's a really easy word to remember. Perhaps that's because it's one of those lovely long, mellifluous words that has not one suffix but two. Like listlessness, wholesomeness and shoeburyness (the sensation you experience when you forget your wellies while walking by the Thames Estuary).

Anyway, it's a particularly bad time of year for forgetting

things so I won't fill your head with any more trivia. You'll find plenty of tips online for helping to remember where you put things, such as filming yourself on your phone as you put them down. Which is great advice – as long as you can remember where you put your phone.

This word was written a month after the 2016 US election.

37

SLADE

If you think 2016 has been a strange sort of year, try 1974. That was the year that saw not one but two General Elections, a hung Parliament, the three-day week, strikes, power cuts, steel plant closures, fuel rationing and inflation at 17.2 per cent. The IRA were at their most deadly, bombing Woolwich, Guildford and Birmingham, the Houses of Parliament and the Tower of London, among other targets. The National Front was on the march and Lord Lucan was on the run.

Away from politics but no less important, Dr Who regenerated from John Pertwee into Tom Baker, World Cup winning England manager Alf Ramsey was sacked, Liverpool messiah Bill Shankly resigned, Brian Clough lasted 44 days at Leeds and Man United were relegated!

Can you imagine a time when there was no Abba? 1974 was the year that they first appeared, winning Eurovision with *Waterloo*.

Yes, 1974 was a truly eventful year and, for many reasons, one that we were all glad to see the back of, but it was bookended by two of the major high points of entertainment history, which happen to be connected by one word:

Slade.

Slade Prison was the fictional setting for *Porridge*, one of the best sitcoms in British history, first aired in September 1974. And Slade was the name of, well, Slade, one of the best bands in British history, who began the year at Number One with the immortal *Merry Xmas Everybody*. We could do with a bit of *Porridge* and Slade now, couldn't we? Both succeeded brilliantly in finding humour in the darkness (literally at times) and put a smile on the nation's faces amid the job losses, power cuts, bombings and riots.

If you're looking for a last-minute present for just about anyone really, I wholeheartedly recommend a copy of *Sladest*, the compilation LP that went straight to the top of the album charts in 1973. My brother bought a copy when it came out, which I 'took care of' when he moved out, and I'm still 'looking after' for him to this day (but don't tell him).

Sladest doesn't include *Merry Xmas Everybody*, which means it's about the only place you won't hear the song this Christmas, but it does feature all five of the band's previous Number Ones, including *Cum On Feel the Noize* and *Skweeze Me, Pleeze Me*, which both went straight to Number One – something no other record had done since The Beatles' *Get Back* in 1969.

Phenomenal.

And it's not just stomping rock; there's the plaintive *Look At Last Nite* and the tender *Coz I Luv You* to vary the mood. Light and shade, pathos, rhetoric, romance, and all those deliberate misspellings... Every home should have it.

Three members of the band turned 70 in 2016. And in a year that saw the Grim Reaper carry out a rather ruthless cull of the entertainment pantheon but leave behind a number of utterly unlovable public figures, whose full capability for sucking the joy out of life remains to be seen, it's comforting to know that we can settle down to our figgy pudding with our loved ones around us, safe in the knowledge that we still have Slade.

Merry Xmas Everybody.

38

SIOUX

L ately I've been reading a lot of philosophical stuff from the mouths of Native Americans. People like Geronimo, Sitting Bull, Crazy Horse and Black Elk. And aside from making me wish that I'd been a bit more imaginative with my kids' names (Send Plenty Snapchat has a nice ring to it), it's convinced me that 2017 is to be the year that I develop a closer affinity with my inner brave. I'm guessing Adam Ant went though a similar epiphany circa 1980.

In a year when it looks like we're going to get our 'leadership' in a maximum of 140 characters and mindfulness and mindlessness go head-to-head, a little Native American wisdom might just offer the protection we need. Eg.,

'It is better to have less thunder in the mouth and more lightning in the hand.' (78 characters)

'The bird who has eaten cannot fly with the bird that is hungry.' (63 characters)

'Silence is the mother of truth, for the silent man is ever to be trusted, while the man ever ready with speech was never taken seriously.' (137 characters)

Now that's what I call a tweet!

Yet it was spoken by a man born nearly 150 years ago, a Lakota Sioux chief by the name of Luther Standing Bear, whose people had a 'no tweeting' policy. In fact, they had a 'no writing' policy, preferring to pass their wisdom from one generation to another by word of mouth. And what words they were! Wigwam, powwow, wampum, Wakan Tanka (the Great Spirit, not rhyming slang for Trump). All those double us... double-Us... double-ewes... Ws... blimey, never try to spell letters!

Of course, the downside to the oral tradition is that you leave yourself vulnerable to other people appropriating your vocabulary and applying their own spellings. Hence the proliferation of tribal names that were clearly written down by Frenchmen, like Cheyenne, Pawnee and Sioux.

Luther Standing Bear was one of the first of his people to get a European-style education and start writing stuff down, thus helping to open people's eyes to the real Native American way of living, their plight at the hands of marauding white settlers and their knack of encapsulating the meaning of life in a pithy sentence or two. In 1902 he toured Britain with Buffalo Bill's Wild West Show, met King Edward VII and fathered what was believed to be the first Native American baby to be born on English soil. Alexandra Standing Bear was named after the Queen of the time but was less fortunate with her middle name – Birmingham – after the place of her birth. At least she wasn't born up the road in Dudley.

But Luther Standing Bear was not altered by his exposure to so-called 'civilisation'. If anything, it served to reinforce his Native principles. "'Civilization'," he wrote, "has been thrust upon me since the days of the reservations, and it has not added one whit to my sense of justice, to my reverence for the rights of life, to my love for truth, honesty and generosity, or to my faith in Wakan Tanka, God of the Lakotas. For after all the great religions have been preached and expounded, or revealed by brilliant scholars, or written in fine books and embellished in fine language with fine covers, man – all man – is still confronted with the Great Mystery.'

Take out the Wakan Tanka bit and that all seems pretty sensible to me.

39

SNOW

The Eskimos have 50 words for it; we have but one: snow, derived from the Old English 'snaw'. And that, you would think, should rule out any ambiguity about a forecast of 'heavy snow'. But it seems not.

Still, who's complaining? Who's really complaining? If we really hated the way snow makes us grind to a halt, slide into one another, spend the night in the office etc, we'd have done something about it years ago. Let's face it, the snow chain was invented in 1904 and you can pick up a set for around 25 quid, but who's got any?

As any self-certified psychologist will tell you, when we don't do anything about a problem it's because, deep down, we actually get some pleasure from it. And there is something delicious about snow chaos, isn't there? It's a great leveller, as Sam Allardyce might say. Sadly for the Scandinavians, they just don't appreciate that, which is why they're so orderly in their management of snow, poor things.

That thing about Eskimos having 50 words for snow isn't an urban myth, by the way. It's not even a rural myth. It's an approximate fact first brought to the attention of the non-Eskimo world by a German-American anthropologist called Franz Boas, who spent a year on Baffin Island assimilating himself with the local Inuits. So thoroughly did Boas throw himself into his work that he wrote in a letter to his fiancée, the American Marie Anna Ernestine Krackowizer, "I am now truly like an Eskimo... living entirely on seal meat."

You can't help wondering what Marie thought. Here's a man who has found himself a prospective wife, proposed to her and secured her acceptance, then sailed off to the frozen North for a year, leaving her at home to prepare for life with an assimilated Eskimo who looked like he was going to be something of an embarrassment at dinner parties.

"Anything Franz doesn't eat, Marie?"

"Um, well, everything but seal really."

Still, the marriage went ahead and they had six children, including one called Hedwig (a girl, by the way, Harry Potter fans), so the rubbing noses bit clearly didn't present a problem.

40

PARANOIA

I don't know what it is about today. I can't help feeling uneasy, like something bad is about to happen. Am I the only one that finds that sign in the Co-op intimidating? You know, the one by the tills that says 'You're Next'?

I had to boycott the inauguration. I said I'd only do it if I could sing *Paranoid* by Black Sabbath but the Donald's people wouldn't have it. They didn't take kindly to the suggestion that the line "Make a joke and I will sigh and you will laugh and I will cry" reminded me of his victory speech.

That legendary song, by the way, was knocked out in a hurry by the band's bassist Geezer Butler, real name Terence Michael Joseph Butler, a vegan, a Villa fan, but definitely not a Satanist. Nor was he paranoid. He just needed a song to finish the album.

Back in 2006, the Institute of Psychiatry at King's College London reported that one in three people in the UK regularly suffers paranoid or suspicious fears. So the paranoiacs are outnumbered two-to-one – that fact alone seems like reason enough to be paranoid. Only when the paranoiacs are in the majority will we begin to cure paranoia.

According to the study, the degrees of paranoia ranged from

thinking people are are saying nasty things about them (40%) to believing there's a conspiracy to do them harm (5%).

Where do you fit in?

Ha! Only joking. No, really. I was joking! Come on…

Joking aside, these figures are alarmingly high. And this study was carried out 10 years ago: pre global financial meltdown, pre Brexit, pre Trump, pre ISIS, pre Putin, pre Bieber… It would be interesting to see the figures today. Especially around 5pm UK time.

The main cause of paranoia, it says here, is the media. This email won't help. Anything that spreads awareness of the rise in paranoia is only going to make people more paranoid. So sorry about that. But you might be thanking me for it soon. As Yossarian said in *Catch-22*, "Just because you're paranoid doesn't meant they aren't after you." A little suspicion saves lives.

Unless you're Stalin, of course, in which case it does the precise opposite. It'll be interesting to see whether the Donald goes the same way as Stalin. Or whether the Russians really did record him doing embarrassing things in a Moscow hotel room and are about to claim their 250 quid and gift us all the greatest ever episode of *You've Been Framed*.

World leaders are particularly prone to paranoia but right now the Donald's demeanour brings to mind a line from Woody Allen's *Deconstructing Harry*: "I don't think you're paranoid. I think you're the opposite of paranoid. I think you walk around with the insane delusion that people like you."

41

DEADLINE

I hate to do this to you but this week all the talk has been about torture. Yes, it's Tax Return deadline time. I was thinking of making this week's word 'revelation' – the euphoric feeling you get when you finally submit your Tax Return to the Inland Revenue and find you've got enough money to pay the bill. But I thought 'deadline' would be a word that more of you could relate to.

There are various claims as to the origin of this relatively modern word. One, as you might have guessed, is from the printing trade, though, as you might not have guessed, it has nothing to do with time limits – that meaning came about a century later. In early 19th century printing, a 'deadline' was a margin around the outside of the page beyond which the type could not be relied upon to render. So a printer would make sure to keep all the key content of the page within the deadline. Makes sense.

Meanwhile, down on the river, anglers were using the term 'dead-line' for a fishing line that was showing no sign of life – quite literally a dead line. You can see the logic in that. Today the same thinking might apply to the line into London Bridge round about 7am. Or what happens to your mobile signal in the vicinity of the Byfleet exit on the A3.

But the most dramatic origin of the word 'deadline' comes

from the American Civil War – specifically the PoW camps. The most notorious of these was Camp Sumter, aka Andersonville, in Georgia, where thousands of Union prisoners died due to the appalling conditions – and the orders of camp commander Heinrich 'Henry' Wirz to shoot anyone who so much as touched the 'deadline'.

In this case the deadline was a boundary around the area occupied by the prisoners, which was sketchy at best and imaginary in parts. With so many men crammed into so small a space, with no shelter from the elements, it was frighteningly easy to find yourself nudged over this deadline, whereupon the guard on the stockade would shoot you. No questions asked.

Wirz was tried, convicted and hanged for his actions at Andersonville, one of only two men to be executed for war crimes during the American Civil War. His was something of a show trial, and it seems he carried the can for the negligence of the Confederate government, but as with all such matters of justice, his big mistake had been to end up on the losing side.

In more favourable circumstances, Wirz would have lived happily ever after as a practitioner of alternative medicine. He'd always wanted to be a doctor but had been forced to leave his native Switzerland due to financial irregularities. Once settled in the US, he was an early adopter of the hydrotherapy revival, practising forms of clinical cleansing by means of high pressure water treatments – yes alright, waterboarding. Perhaps this is evidence that there's a fine line between a homeopath and a psychopath.

Wirz, aged just 42, met his final deadline on 10 November 1865 and took a while to die at the end of the rope. Unpleasant, but slightly less painful than filing his Tax Return.

42

STRESS

I know… the last thing you need at the end of a stressful week is another email. According to extensive scientific research, we're suffering more stress today than at any other time in history. Quite how they know is unclear, but according to the *Daily Mail*… ok, sorry, forget that.

There is proper research, though, that says stress levels are at an all time high. Things like email, social media, money, work, politics, public transport and the continuing existence of Piers Morgan are driving our stress hormone levels through the roof, but is this really worse than in the days when 'workplace angst' meant being skewered on the tusk of a woolly mammoth? Which would you rather be pestered by: spam emails or a sabre-toothed tiger? Given the choice between waiting for a wild boar to wander within range of your spear and waiting for the 7.07 at East Croydon Station, which do you think would be more likely to keep you awake at night?

Nevertheless, the experts claim that, while our ancestors may have been more physically stressed, they were much less mentally stressed than we are. Sadly, we have no historical evidence against which to test this, unless you count Channel 5's 10,000 BC. And that in itself could be proof that the scientists are right. The fact that the ancients left us profound philosophical arguments and complex calculations involving the internal angles of a heptagon, but no recorded research into general stress levels, suggests that it wasn't really an issue in those days.

But when you look at the main causes of stress today, you can't say the Romans, for example, weren't exposed to the same pressures: money, work, status, politics, gossip, war, sandals... OK, so they didn't have email hackers but they did have the Visigoths.

They had a word for stress too – strictus – from which we get all sorts of stressful words: strain, strict, distress, stringent, strung...

And here's another argument: the modern day antidote to stress – mindfulness meditation – is 3,500 years old. So it's fair to assume there must have been a stress problem going on in India in 1,500BC. Otherwise, why invent yoga?

So I've been studying mindfulness in order to overcome my own modern day stresses, like getting Word of the Week emails out on time every Friday, and I have to say it's fascinating stuff. Now that we don't go to church as part of our regular routine, we've forgotten how to be still and unoccupied for any length of time, or to pay attention to the present without being distracted by thoughts of anxiety (future) or regret (past). By retraining your brain to be mindful, you learn that most of your stress is caused by thoughts rather than facts and, therefore, the threats that cause you stress are, in fact, non-existent.

It takes a bit of working out and, to be honest, I don't think I'm quite there with it yet. For example, this morning I learnt that I don't actually exist, which rather took the wind out of my sails.

Still, back next week, hopefully – all being well.

43

HYGGE

If you're an avid reader of trendy style magazines (of course you are), you will have come across this word some time ago. "Oh pu-lease!" I hear you tut, "that hygge is so last year!" If that's you, well done. I doff my cap. If not, let me take a moment to explain.

Hygge, as you may have guessed, is a foreign word – Danish, to be precise – and it's a tricky one to pronounce. Say 'hig' and you'll be laughed out of Vogue House faster than you can say, "I'm spending the weekend at daddy's country estate in Berkshire." Sources differ as to the correct pronunciation. It could be 'hue-urrgh', in which case I remember it being a major talking point around 11.30pm outside the Croydon pubs I used to frequent in the 80s. Or it could be 'hoo-gar'. I prefer the latter as it provides poets and songwriters with that lyrical Holy Grail – a word to rhyme with nougat.

I feel a Cliff Richard Christmas single coming on.

But even more tricky than the pronunciation is the literal translation of hygge. Whole armies of wordsmiths have tried and failed. It's like trying to find another word for thesaurus. The closest anyone has come is probably cosiness, but that doesn't even tell half the story. Hygge is about togetherness, relaxation, hospitality, comfort, warmth, intimacy and, yes, cosiness. It is a feeling, a style, a philosophy, a handy way to fill eight pages of an interior design magazine.

The chief ingredients appear to be candles, pastries and cycling, with the occasional cardigan and perhaps a Val Doonican record thrown in. Apparently these are what the Danes regard as the good things in life. Whatever happened to horned helmets and pillage, that's what I want to know?

The beauty of the English language is that it offers/proffers/provides/extends a choice/selection/menu/range of words for just about everything you want to say/convey/express. Having said that, there is usually one word for every situation/instance/scenario that is more apt/appropriate/apposite than the rest. It's the subtle nuances that make the choosing of words such a pleasure.

If we look back over history, the usual form when coming across a foreign word that we can't translate literally is just to adopt that word and call it English. Zeitgeist, chic, schadenfreude, Gibraltar… All ours. So expect to see hygge adopted into the Oxford English Dictionary before long.

And if you haven't yet decked your home with candles and knitwear, hung a bike on the wall and filled the air with the evocative aroma of freshly baked pastries and herrings, what in the name of Frigg* are you waiting for?

*The Norse goddess of soft furnishings.

44

SAVELOY

The sun is shining, the mercury's touching double figures, it's Friday, my bike just passed its MoT and I've got a saveloy. Does life get any better than this?

It's traditional to visit the chippy on a Friday, even though, contrary to popular belief, Friday wasn't called Friday because it's the day for deep-fat frying. As anyone who's currently reading a book about English history will tell you, it got its name from those marauding Norsemen who took it upon themselves to colonise England in the latter years of the first millennium AD. When they weren't setting fire to things and using mild-mannered clerics for archery practice, they liked to unwind by thinking up names for the days of the week. In this case they named the day after their goddess Frigg, aka Freya (incidentally the only Norse goddess to make it into this blog two weeks running).

It's a mysterious sausage, the saveloy. Certainly more of a southern delicacy than a northern one, it's never sat comfortably among the gravy and mushy peas. Indeed, celebrated Macclesfield songsters the Macc Ladds once saw fit to sing of a visit to London, 'No gravy at the chippy, and what's a saveloy?' So let's shed a little light on this spicy assemblage of reconstituted pig meat.

The name 'saveloy' (and, therefore, presumably the sausage

itself, since I can't think of anything else that goes by the name saveloy) dates back to 1837, when someone took the French word 'cervelas' and mispronounced it. The French took cervelas from the Italian 'cervellata', a derivation of the Italian 'cervello', which owed its origin to the Latin 'cerebrum'.

You don't have to be a brain surgeon to see where this is going.

Yep, the original saveloy was made from pigs' brains. Which makes you stop and think mid-chew, doesn't it? Maybe it still is. Who knows? The ingredients are vague. Pork meat could mean anything, couldn't it? The cannibals of New Guinea believed that when you eat someone else's brain you acquire some of their intelligence. Come to think of it, I am quite messy and I can smell a truffle at fifty yards.

In trying to unearth some historical information about saveloys (why has no-one written a book on the subject?), the best I could find was this intriguing snippet on Wikipedia:

At the turn of the 20th century, the saveloy was described in an Australian court case as a "highly seasoned dry sausage originally made of brains, but now young pork, salted".

I know what you're thinking: what on earth was that court case about? I wish I could tell you but, alas, we can only speculate. Like so many things where saveloys are concerned, it was left hanging.

45

QUIZ

Apologies to anyone who opened this email expecting to find a quiz. We do love a quiz, don't we, us Brits? True or False: In any given week you can find more than 300 different quiz shows on British TV. I include in that *Good Morning Britain*, in which there is only one question and it's always the same: Why the hell do people keep giving Piers Morgan work?

No sooner was BBC TV past its second birthday than it began broadcasting its first TV quiz show, *Spelling Bee*, in 1938. This, as the name suggests, was a spelling quiz, in which teams of soberly dressed B-listers wearing headphones were given words and asked to – wait for it – spell them. You could almost taste the excitement.

It was not the BBC's finest hour but it did gain some traction in the public consciousness (well, the five people who owned a telly anyway) as an alternative to watching dust gather in the grate. Eventually Neville Chamberlain was forced to declare war on Germany just to get it off air.

But *Spelling Bee* tapped into a strange part of the British psyche that has turned us into a nation of quizaholics. And it's not just a case of wanting to air our knowledge of trivia. Each week, three million people tune in to *University Challenge* to watch other people answer questions they don't understand.

It's a far cry from the first pub quiz I ever went to. Back in the mid-80s, when London's Docklands was a flat no-man's land roamed by dinosaurs and drooling developers, a wind-blown wasteland of empty waterways, pile drivers and the occasional Victorian terrace that had yet to succumb to the wrecking ball, there stood just two commercial buildings: the office I worked in and a pub, frequented by my workmates, the local psychopath and a bunch of resentful ex-dockers. In an effort to boost trade and build bridges between her eclectic clientele, the landlady decided to put on a quiz night. Question 1: What are you looking at? (We didn't get to Question 2.)

Ironically, the one question that nobody has yet been able to answer is 'Where does the word quiz come from?' You would assume it derived from the Latin 'quizzicus', wouldn't you? Or perhaps an Old English word for the wrong end of a pig. But it doesn't. There is no Latin word 'quizzicus'. There's a good story, which appears to have some validity, about a Dublin theatre owner coining the word to win a bet that he could invent a new word and get the whole city using it within a day. But there is also prior evidence of the word being used to mean both an eccentric person (from which we get the word quizzical) and a type of toy like a yo-yo.

This was in the late 1700s. It wasn't until the mid-19th century that the verb 'to quiz' came about, meaning to question. And even then no-one seemed to know where it came from. So if you opened this email hoping for questions, I'd like to think I've delivered. If not, here are three more that cost me dear last night.

Is Australia a continent?

Really? Since when?

46

SPRING

This Wednesday a cry came out of a corner of the office, "It's the first day of Spring!" To which we replied, "Spring doesn't take a capital letter, unless it's at the start of a sentence or in a title, of course." To which the cry came back, "I didn't say spring with a capital letter, and anyway, it's not the first day of actual spring." That's the kind of uncertainty that unsettles the human spirit.

So come on, when does spring start? Is it when the first daffodil flowers on the roof of the Met Office? Is it when the mad frogwoman of Little Piddlington emerges from her pond and wanders into the Co-op to buy her first 5-pack of Creme Eggs? Is it when the Earth's 23.5 degree tilt on its rotational axis in relation to its orbit round the sun renders day and night of equal length? Do they even have daffodils on the roof of the Met Office?

It's one of those questions that the great minds of humanity really should have settled by now. They can calculate Pi, put a man on the moon and invent a toastie that goes in the toaster, but they can't tell us definitively when spring starts, or whether or not Australia is a continent, or is it Australasia or Oceania, and if it's just Australia, where does that leave New Zealand? Incontinent?

It's no good asking the Met Office. "Depending upon which definition you use, there are actually two different dates that mark the first day of spring," is all they can say. This is the sort of fluffy prevarication you get when you look to scientists for answers. Creationists may all be mad as cheese but at least they pick an argument and stick to it.

So there's meteorological spring, which is dictated by the arrangement of the months: quite simply, March 1 – May 31; and there's astronomical spring, set by the position of the Earth in relation to the Sun, beginning with the vernal equinox on March 20/21, when night and day are of equal length, and ending with the summer solstice on June 21/22, the longest day. But the summer solstice is midsummer's day, so how can that be the end of spring?

Ridiculous.

The word spring, as a seasonal concept, came into the English language as 'springing time', a lovely, descriptive 14th century expression, taken from the German springelfolstrumphentische and clearly inspired by the things that were going on at that time of year: streams flowing, buds bursting, lambs birthing, that kind of stuff… Which is all very fluid and moveable from one year to the next and so, therefore, should we not say spring begins when we all agree that it feels a bit springy, rather than when some wishy-washy theorist with a telescope dictates?

And why isn't spring spelt with a capital letter? Because, for some reason the seasons are not deemed to be proper nouns, which reinforces the argument that they are more of a feeling than a thing.

So enjoy the rest of winter, folks. And keep your wits about you in the Co-op.

47

SO

So I was thinking, the title 'Word of the Week' doesn't really do justice to this multifunctional little number. I know we're only a few years in but it has to be a candidate for Word of the Millennium. Having spent most of its life barely noticed amid the infinitives, gerunds and transferred epithets, 'so' has enjoyed such a remarkable renaissance in recent years that you can barely go two minutes without hearing it. It's the verbal equivalent of Mary Berry.

'So' has always been a versatile word, able to do a job as an adverb, adjective, pronoun or conjunction. Then, some time around the turn of the millennium, people started using 'so' to turn nouns into adjectives. 'That's so last century.'

Clever.

But that wasn't the end of it. Having discovered that this dinky amalgamation of two of the more unremarkable letters of the alphabet had hidden powers, linguistic pioneers began to use it at the beginning of their sentences, like a conjunction between the new sentence and a non-existent preceding sentence.

'So I've just been to the shops.'

The effect was dynamite. By cunningly putting 'so' at the

beginning of a brand new conversation, you could create the impression that you had already been talking and that the listener must have missed something. 'So' became part of the New Labour Third Way of Speaking, which involved putting extraneous words at the beginning of sentences, purely to draw attention to yourself, buy time and sound a bit patronising.

If you've hung on to all your old videos of Tony Blair interviews, keep the kids amused tonight by replaying them and counting how many times he begins his answers with 'Look'. They'll be asleep in seconds.

So, what does 'so' mean?

It can mean lots of things: very, therefore, thus, for that reason, in order that, as stated… lots of things. But there's one thing that 'so' does not mean and that's 'a needle pulling thread'. Sorry to disappoint you, *Sound of Music* fans, but what Maria should have sung was 'Sol – a bottle of Mexican beer'. But that doesn't rhyme with 'jam and bread', so it really would have brought her back to do, do, do, doh!

The sol-fa scale – Do, Re, Mi, Fa, Sol, La, Ti, Do – as used on the Continent instead of our A, B, C, D, E, F, G designation for the musical notes, was invented by a sixth century Benedictine monk called Guido d'Arezzo. He had been charged by the Archbishop of Seville with finding a way to write music down so it wouldn't be lost in the mists of time.

He decided to employ an ancient Indian technique of assigning syllables to each note of the scale and used for his key a hymn called *Ut Queant Laxis*, which goes (altogether now):

Ut queant laxis
resonare fibris
Mira gestorum
famuli tuorum,
Solve polluti
labii reatum,
Sancte Iohannes.

The Ut and Si were later changed to Do and Ti in some languages, much to the relief, no doubt, of Rogers and Hammerstein, who would otherwise have been left with something like this.

Ut a word, a funny little word
Re a drop of golden sun
Mi a name I call myself
Fa a long, long way to run
Sol a bottle of Mexican beer
La a note to follow Sol
Si a wet thing full of fish
Which will being us back to Ut, Ut, Ut, Ut...

So that's not quite as snappy, is it?

48

LISP

S ay what you like about sausages, they don't make life easy when you've got a lisp. Neither do crisps, Wispa bars, biscuits or any of the other sweet tasting sensations they sell in the shops. Oh yes, life with a lisp can be cruel.

But the cruellest thing of all is the word lisp itself. I mean, what joker came up with a word for the inability to pronounce S sounds properly and put an S in the middle of it? Samson the Sadducee Strangler? Silus the Syrian Assassin? Some silly sod, whoever it was.

It doesn't end there either. The more you investigate the lisp phenomenon, the more you come across words like sibilance (the deliberate use of consecutive S sounds to give everyone a laugh at the expense of lispers – hilarious) and learn that a lisp is caused by the way the tongue touches the teeth. Try saying that without spraying spittle over your thesis on photosynthesis in thistles.

I'm not afraid to admit that I had a strong lisp as a child. I first became aware of it when asked to sing *Sing a Song of Sixpence* solo in school and nearly pushed my front teeth out. After that I became so self-conscious that I avoided words with Ss in them for 10 years until, on turning 16, I plucked up the courage to whisper the word 'sex' to a sixth form girl from Sissinghurst and was sniggered out of the snug bar at the Swan and Sugarloaf.

I'm aware that this is becoming uncomfortably autobiographical. Stay with it.

By this stage I'd been listening intently to The Clash for several years, for ciphers to the riddles and reasons to the rhymes, and suddenly it dawned on me why I liked the band so much. Joe Strummer had a lisp! It was endearing. It was characterful. I decided to stop trying to conceal my lisp and within two weeks I'd landed myself a Spanish girlfriend. It crossed my mind that I'd spent the first 20 years of my life speaking the wrong language for my tongue.

The love affair didn't last – Spain is a hell of a commute – but the job was done. My lispophobia was cured. OK, so people I meet for the first time still think my name is Thim (even though that's not a real name) but at least I can pronounce chorizo properly, and when you live in Reigate that's an asset you can't put a price on.

So celebrate with me, fellow lispers, as we approach the start of astronomical spring, and remember to send your sympathies to the lispless.

They don't know what they're mithing.

49

CHUCK

Nobody seems prepared to identify the one true father of rock'n'roll but, as the obits pointed out this week, there's a strong likelihood that it was Chuck Berry. It certainly has his looks.

I don't talk about this a lot but I actually played a key part in Chuck's greatest success – and possibly his downfall. You see, the first record I ever bought was Chuck's one and only Number One. No, not *Maybellene*. Not *Roll Over Beethoven*. Not *Memphis, Tennessee*. In fact, not any of the rock'n'roll classics that inspired The Beatles, Stones, Beach Boys et al. We're talking about the 1972 novelty record *My Ding-a-Ling*.

I bought it as part of a three-way syndicate with my brother and sister, pooling our pocket money and thus helping to catapult the alleged father of rock'n'roll to the rightful chart-topping spot that had, for some reason, been denied him up to that point (possibly something to do with his frequent spells behind bars, for armed robbery, transporting minors across county lines and tax evasion).

To be fair, the lion's share of the credit should probably go to the infamous guardian of the nation's morals Mary Whitehouse, who tried to get the record banned on the BBC, thus ensuring that every liberal-minded person rushed out and bought it. Plus a large number of unliberal-minded campanologists, who thought that at last here was a song about bell-ringing.

It's funny how the years concertina as you get older. To a six-year-old in 1972, Chuck Berry seemed like an old man. Today that would be like calling Atomic Kitten a bunch of old women. Or dismissing Steps as a long-forgotten blip with no lasting influence on cultural history.

Ahem.

What is remarkable, given his lifestyle, is that Chuck did live to be an old man, so much so that when news of his passing was announced this week, a lot of people responded, "I didn't realise he was still alive." To which the flippant reply would have been, "He's not." But that would have been missing the point. For a wayward rock'n'roller, 90 is a damn good innings. Perhaps we should all forget the yoga and pilates and start doing the duck walk on a daily basis.

Anyway, the point I'm trying to come to, in a Southern Rail replacement bus service kind of way, is that Chuck is a funny thing to call a person, when you think of all the other meanings of the word. To throw or hurl; an illegal bowling action in cricket; an involuntary projection of your burger from stomach to train window; the ending of a relationship. In the 16th century 'chuck' meant to punch somebody under the chin. Not particularly endearing. As with most 16th century pasttimes, this has been moderated over the centuries into more of a playful touch, usually applied to babies and toddlers, but still annoying.

Then there's the bit on the end of a drill that holds the bit… on the end of a drill. And there's the cut of beef that's usually chopped into lumps for stewing, both of which are believed to have evolved as a variation of the word chunk. Still struggling to find anything you would want to be named after.

A North American marmot with a heavy body and short legs? No thanks. Cowboy food? I'll pass. Ah, but what's this? A term of endearment popular in the late 16th century, derived from the word chick? Now that's more like it.

Shakespeare used it several times in his plays, most notably in an exchange between Macbeth and Lady Macbeth. "Be innocent of the knowledge, dearest chuck," he says to her, in an effort to cocoon her from the dastardly deed he's about to perform but sounding more Cilla than killer. Antony uses the same pet name for Cleopatra. Anyone would think they'd all been watching *Blind Date*.

None of which explains why Chuck became the short form of Charles. Lady Macbeth's first name wasn't Charles, as far as we know. Neither was Cleo's, nor Antony's for that matter, otherwise Shakespeare would have called the play Charles and Charles.

But just as there's a trend for turning surnames into nicknames by adding 'y' to the end – Jonesy, Smithy, Rooney…y – our ancestors created nicknames by shortening first names with an abrupt 'k' or 'ck' – monosyllabic 'k' sounds being popular among speakers of germanic languages, especially when they were trying to wind up their Norman overlords. So we got Jack from John, Rick from Richard, Mick from Michael… and in later years Chuck from Charles.

I had a rummage through my singles collection to see if I still had that copy of *My Ding-a-Ling*. They're fetching all of 99p on Ebay. It had gone. Someone must have chucked it out.

50

CHIT

Alright, stop tittering at the back. There's nothing amusing about the word chit, any more than there is about other everyday gardening terms, such as butt, harden off or dibber. Now pay attention, here's a question for you: what connects a potato to a big cat? (And no, the answer isn't gaffer tape, although that probably would work.)

The answer, in case you haven't guessed yet, is the word chit. Chitting is bang in vogue right now. As any potato enthusiast knows, if you haven't chitted by the end of March you may have left it too late. For those who don't grow, chitting is the process of encouraging potatoes to sprout before you sow them. It makes them grow faster and gives a better crop, you see?

So if you're passing the allotments and you overhear someone saying they've come down with the chitters, don't be alarmed. It just means they've arrived with the seed potatoes. You can lean confidently on the fence and cheerfully join in with something like, "Aye, and you should see the size of my pink fir apples."

So that's what chit means. It comes from an old English term for a small sprout, and prior to that the young of an animal, from which we also get the expression "a chit of a girl", a phrase we've been using to dismiss young, insolent girls since the early 17th century.

"And the cat?" I hear you ask wearily. Ah yes, the cat.

When I was at school and we were given an official letter to take home to our parents, we'd be told to "come back with the chits" the next day. It always got a laugh, apart from the time Paul ____ took the joke literally and they had to close the canteen for a week. The chit (or chitty) in this instance was the small, tear-off strip of paper at the bottom of the letter, which your parents would sign to say they were happy for you to go to Lullingstone Roman Villa and wouldn't complain if the school happened not to bring you back, or words to that effect.

I always assumed chitty was a term of endearment for a chit, just as kitty is for a cat (that's not the connection, by the way – it's much better than that) but it was, in fact, a word brought back from India in the 18th century, along with chutney and bungalows. It was derived from the Hindi 'chitthi' (pronounced 'chitthi'), meaning a letter or note. This in turn came from 'chitra-s', which was an old Sanskrit word meaning 'distinctively marked'.

I feel I'm rushing to the conclusion now. I want to hold it back and build up the anticipation but I suspect you might already have guessed the connection. OK, here goes.

From that Sanskrit word, via various metamorphoses, we get...

Cheetah!

Isn't that amazing? So there's your connection: from potatoes to big cats in one seamless stream of cobblers. And if you're reading this tomorrow, remember to plant your spuds facing north-east. They taste better that way.

51

PILGRIM

You may be experiencing a sense of déjà vu. I will explain. Last week's Word of the Week was something of a red herring. The subject line of the email said the word was pilgrim but the actual word was chit. There then followed a stream of what can only be described as chitchat. The management would like to apologise for any distress this may have caused. We put it down to the fact that it was late on a Friday evening and the writer had probably been on the Pilgrim* at the time.

*Pilgrim Ale is the local Reigate brew, and very palatable it is too. The name alludes to the pilgrims who historically travelled this way between Winchester and Canterbury to visit the shrine of Thomas à Beckett. Why they started at Winchester I don't know. Perhaps they'd gone there by mistake, not having paid attention in History. The road they took is called The Pilgrim's Way, so there was no excuse for going astray a second time.

Winchester to Canterbury, a walk of around 120 miles through leafy countryside and gentle topography, is one of the less demanding of the many pilgrimages of many faiths that take place around the world. My mother-in-law, for example, once walked for six weeks all the way from Gaudonville in SW France, over the Pyrenees and across to Santiago de Compostela in NW Spain, which is pretty valiant by any standards. We only sent her out for a loaf of bread.

So where does the word pilgrim come from? Interestingly, it's from the Latin word 'peregrinus' – a person from elsewhere, a foreigner – which you will immediately, and correctly, conclude has something to do with the peregrine falcon. Falco peregrinus was given its name by 13th century German philosopher and saint (how do you apply for a job like that?) Albertus Magnus (Big Albert), in reference to the fact that young birds were captured during their migration rather than taken from the nest. Easier apparently.

Of course, Falco peregrinus takes the first part of its name not from Mark Falco, the Spurs striker of the 1980s, but from the Austrian singer, whose hit single *Rock Me Amadeus* topped the UK charts in 1988 (so chances are at least one of you bought it. Come on, own up). Did you know, by the way, that Falco had died in a car crash with a bus in the Dominican Republic in 1998? Neither did I.

Ah well. Last week, the word chit led us to cheetah, the fastest mammal on Earth – but not as fast, it turns out, as the peregrine falcon, which can dive at speeds of up to 242mph. Frankly, though, if plummeting out of the sky is a valid criterion for measuring an animal's speed, then surely one of those goats they chuck off that tower in Spain each year must be faster than a cheetah by the time it hits the Dunlopillo. And what about that bloke who leapt out of a balloon in space? I bet he overtook a few falcons on the way down.

If you want to know what 200mph+ feels like, watch this amazing video[5]. This is Guy Martin chasing champion road racer Michael Dunlop, who I had the pleasure of interviewing this week, round the Isle of Man TT course, where he holds the lap record. It makes me think I really must try to get more out of my scooter. My mother-in-law's average speed was 2mph, so no land speed records there. But then she did have the Pyrenees to contend with.

52

TELEBANTER

This Word of the Week thing has been going on long enough now that, like a pub singer who churns out the crowd pleasers every night, I'm beginning to tire of other people's words and feel it's time for a word of my own. So, ladies and gentlemen, I give you…

…Telebanter!

I'm surprised no-one has beaten me to this word. It's very much a word for our time. It means, quite simply, banter at a distance – noun or verb – from the English 'banter', meaning 'banter', and the Greek 'tele', meaning 'far off' (though in the case of the Teletubbies, never far off enough).

You may have come across the word 'telecommute'. To telecommute is to work from home, whether in inverted commas or otherwise. It's an interesting example of how language evolves and mutates into new forms. We understand 'commute' to mean 'travel to work', so 'to travel to work at a distance' suggests a bizarre performance of trying to get to work but never actually managing to come close. You might refer to it as Southern Rail.

But commute didn't originally mean to travel, it meant to change, as in commuting a prison sentence into something lighter.

Commuters as we know them originated in the US as a nickname for folks holding a 'commutation ticket', or a season ticket, for getting the streetcar to work. This ticket took its name from the sense of changing one type of payment into another.

Anyway, for all the benefits of working from home – no stressful journeys, seeing more of the kids, keeping on top of the gardening etc – the downside is that you miss out on the office chat. Never underestimate the value of office chat. It bonds, it cheers, it inspires. A few years ago, irritatingly young Yahoo CEO Marissa Meyer banned her staff from working from home for that very reason. There weren't enough ideas being exchanged over the water cooler and the jokes about Gordon from Accounts were drying up. There followed some notable improvements in Yahoo's performance and the office jokes got measurably funnier.

But Meyer was swimming against the tide. Two thirds of the workforce now 'work from home' to some extent and none of them have expressed a desire to 'put the lawnmower back in the shed'. So the problem facing modern day employers is not so much "Should I allow my staff to work from home?" as "How will I make sure they maintain the office banter?"

Enter telebanter – the art of bantering from a distance.

Don't get me wrong, I haven't invented telebanter per se, I've just invented the word. I don't even like it that much, to be honest. I just think it's necessary. Like a feral cat that eats the scraps from your bins and coughs up fur balls on your slippers, Telebanter® has been around for too long without having a name. We've been doing it via email for years – usually with disastrous results – and now you've got WhatsApp to keep your employees bantering long after they've all gone home. With telebanter you never have to feel cut off from work again.

You have to be careful, though. I could tell you the story of R_____, who got his WhatsApp groups muddled up recently and inadvertently sent a message to the entire office effectively telling the boss's wife to get a move on on the toilet – only not in those words. Laugh? How we laughed! And the next day productivity increased by 2% and the office jokes were 7% funnier.

OPTIONAL LINKS

We all know that print and hyperlinks make uncomfortable bedfellows. I promise you, however, that if you take the trouble to key in these links they will take you to places you will never forget. Remember not to leave any gaps.

[1] http://www.gettyimages.co.uk/detail/photo/map-making-high-res-stock-photography/HS4869-001
[2] https://www.theguardian.com/uk-news/video/2014/apr/21/world-marble-championships-germany-britain-video
[3] http://www.kentarchaeology.ac/cassets/KentishDialect.pdf
[4] https://www.youtube.com/watch?v=ZPVg1y6vMSw
[5] https://www.youtube.com/watch?v=OmNXCJt7K3Q

SO WHAT NEXT?

Word of the Week is an ongoing project. A second volume will be published if there's enough interest in this one, and in the meantime you can keep up to date by subscribing to the weekly emails at

WWW.BALANCEMEDIA.CO.UK/BLOG

Here you can also trawl through the archives for any words you might have missed. You can follow Word of the Week on Twitter.

@WORD_OFTHEWEEK

That just leaves me to thank you for reading this collection of words. I hope you made it last.